Chasseur of 1914

Chasseur of 1914

Experiences of the Twilight of French Light Cavalry by a Young Officer During the Early Battles of the Great War in Europe

Marcel Dupont

Chasseur of 1914: Experiences of the Twilight of French Light Cavalry by a Young Officer During the Early Battles of the Great War in Europe

by Marcel Dupont

First published in 1916 under the title
In the Field

Published by Leonaur Ltd

ISBN (10 digit): 1-84677-112-9 (hardcover)
ISBN (13 digit): 978-1-84677-112-5 (hardcover)

ISBN (10 digit): 1-84677-111-0 (softcover)
ISBN (13 digit): 978-1-84677-111-8 (softcover)

http://www.leonaur.com

Publisher's Notes

In the interests of authenticity, the spellings, grammar and place names used have been retained from the original editions.

The opinions of the authors represent a view of events in which he was a participant related from his own perspective, as such the text is relevant as an historical document.

The views expressed in this book are not necessarily those of the publisher.

To

General Cherfils

A Tribute of Sincere Gratitude

Contents

Preface

In the following pages the reader will find no tactical studies, no military criticism, no vivid picture of a great battle. I have merely tried to make a written record of some of the hours I have lived through during the course of this war. A modest Lieutenant of Chasseurs, I cannot claim to form any opinion as to the operations which have been carried out for the last nine months on an immense front. I only speak of things I have seen with my own eyes, in the little corner of the battlefield occupied by my regiment.

It occurred to me that if I should come out of the deathly struggle safe and sound, it would be a pleasure to me some day to read over these notes of battle or bivouac. I thought, further, that my people would be interested in them. So I tried to set down my impressions in my intervals of leisure. Days of misery, days of joy, days of battle.... What volumes one might write, if one were to follow our squadrons day by day in their march!

I preferred to choose among many memories. I did not wish to compose memoirs, but only to evoke the most tragic or the most touching moments of my campaign. And, indeed, I have had only too many from which to choose.

I shall rejoice if I have been able to revive some phases of the tragedy in which we were the actors for my brothers-in-arms.

Further, I gladly offer these "impressions" to any non-combatants they may interest. They must not look for the talents of a great story-teller, nor the thrilling interest of a novel. All they will find is the simple tale of an eyewitness, the unschooled effort of a soldier more apt with the sword than with the pen.

Marcel Dupont

Chapter 1
How I Went to the Front
August, 1914

The train was creeping along slowly in the soft night air. Seated on a truss of hay in the horse-box with my own two horses and that of my orderly, Wattrelot, I looked out through the gap left by the unclosed sliding door. How slowly we were going! How often we stopped! I got impatient as I thought of the hours we were losing whilst the other fellows were fighting and reaping all the glory. Station after station we passed; bridges, level crossings, tunnels. Everywhere I saw soldiers guarding the line and the bayonets of the old chassepôts glinting in the starlight. Now and again the train would suddenly pull up for some mysterious reason. The three horses, frightened at being brought into collision with each other, made the van echo to the thunder of their hoofs as they slipped, stamped, and recovered their balance. I got up to calm them with soothing words and caresses. By the light of the wretched lantern swinging and creaking above the door I could see their three heads, with pricked ears and uneasy eyes. They were breathing hard and could not understand why they had been brought away from their comfortable stable with its thick litter of clean straw. They were not thinking about the war, but they seemed to understand that their good times were over, that they would have to resign themselves to all sorts of discomforts, march unceasingly, pass nights in camps under the pouring rain, keep their heavy equipment on their backs for many days together, and not always get food when they were hungry.

Then the train would set off again with a noise of tightened couplings and creaking waggons. Whilst I was mechanically looking out at the darkness, dotted here and there with the coloured lights of the signals placed along the line, my straying thoughts would wander to the fields of battle and try to picture the scene on my arrival at the Front.

It was the 28th of August, nearly a month after the order had been given for mobilisation. And the armies had been fighting for some days already. What had happened? We could only glean part of the truth from the short official announcements. We knew there had been hard fighting at Charleroi, at Dinant, and in the direction of Nancy. But the result had not been defined. I thought I could guess, however, that these battles had not been decisive, but that they had cost both sides dear. I was tempted to rejoice, fool that I was, to think that the first great victories would not be won before I joined my regiment. I had not yet been able to console myself for the ill-fortune that prevented me from starting with the squadrons of the first line. And yet I had to submit to regulations. The colonel was inflexible, and answered my entreaties by quoting the inexorable rule: In every cavalry regiment the sixth lieutenant in order of seniority must stay at the depôt to help the major and the captain of the 5th squadron. They must assemble, equip, and train the reserve squadrons of the regiment.

I shall never forget what those days were to me. Days of overwhelming work, when, in a tropical heat, I was busy from sunrise to sunset, entering the names of thousands of men, registering the horses, giving certificates, and providing food for the lot. It needed some skill to find billets for them all; the horses were lodged in stables, riding establishments and yards, the men in every corner and nook of the vast district. It was tiresome work, and would have been almost impossible but for the general goodwill and admirable discipline. But all the time I was thinking of the fellows away in Belgium boldly reconnoitring the masses of Germans and coming into contact with the enemy.

At last, at eleven o'clock on the 28th of August, the colonel's telegram came ordering me to go at once and replace my young friend, Second-Lieutenant de C., seriously wounded whilst reconnoitring. At six o'clock in the evening I had packed my food, strapped on my kit, and got my horses into the train. I set off with a light heart, and my fellow-officers of the Reserve and of the Territorials, who were still at the depôt, came to see me off.

But how slowly the train travelled, and what a long way off our little garrison town in the west seemed to me when I thought of the firing line out towards the north! I made up my mind to try to imitate my faithful Wattrelot, who had been snoring in peace for ever so long. I stretched myself on the golden straw and waited impatiently for the dawn, dozing and dreaming.

At about eight o'clock in the morning the train stopped at the concentration station of N. What a crowd, and yet what order and precision in this formidable traffic! All the commissariat trains for the army muster here before being sent off to different parts of the Front. The numerous sidings were all covered with long rows of trucks. In every direction engines getting up steam were panting and puffing. In the middle of this hurly-burly men were on the move, some of them calm, jaded and patient. These were the railwaymen, who went about in a business-like way, pushing railway vans, counting packages, carrying papers, checking lists, and giving information politely and willingly. The rest were soldiers, lost, bewildered in the midst of this entanglement of lines which seemed inextricable. They were asking each other questions, swearing, laughing, protesting, and then they got into a train and were promptly hauled out and sent to another. But, with all this, there was no disorder, no lack of discipline. Everywhere the same admirable composure reigned that I had already noticed at the station of my little garrison town.

With Wattrelot's help, I tidied myself up for a visit to the military authorities of the station. After many difficulties, and after passing through the hands of a number of sentries and orderlies on duty, I came into the presence of a kindly captain, to whom I stated my case: "These are my marching orders, Captain; I am to join the—Light Cavalry. Do you know where it is just now?" The captain raised his hands to Heaven with a look of despair: "How am I to know where any regiment is now? You can't expect it. All I can do for you is to couple your truck on to the commissariat train of your army corps. It will take you as far as the terminus, and there you must see what you can do."

I went back to my horses. After various excursions hither and thither which took up the whole morning I at last managed to get my horse-box coupled to the train. Wattrelot and I, together with the Territorial section that served as guard, were the only passengers. The whole train was composed of vans stuffed with food supplies and mysterious cases, packed into some separate vans carefully sealed. Our departure was fixed for two o'clock, and meanwhile I had a chat with the Territorial lieutenant who commanded our escort. I tried to find out from him what had happened at the Front. He did not know any more than I did, and merely told me how sorry he was for his own ill-luck: "You know, our job is no joke. We start after luncheon, travel all the rest of the day and part of the night, sleep where we can, and the next day we go back again in the empty train. It takes still longer to get back. And the day after we begin all over again."

And the worthy man quietly folded his hands on the "fair roundness" of his figure. He looked a good sort of fellow. He did his job conscientiously; put his men into the third-class compartments assigned to them; saw that they had their cartridges, and gave them some fatherly counsel; and then he invited me into the second-class compartment reserved for him. But I declined, as I preferred to travel with my horses. The train jolted off. The heat was tropical. We had pushed our sliding-door wide open, and, seated on our packages, we contemplated the smiling summer landscape as it passed slowly before us. And I came to the conclusion that we had found out the pleasantest way of travelling:—to have a railway carriage to yourself, where you can stand up, walk about and lie down; to go at a pace that allows you to enjoy the scenery of the countries you pass through; and to be able to linger and admire such and such a view, such and such a country mansion or monument of olden days! That is a hundred times better than the shaking and rush of a train de luxe .

I was delighted and touched by the sympathetic interest shown in us by the people. Everywhere old men, women and children waved their handkerchiefs and called out, "Good luck!... Good luck!"

The worthy Territorials answered back as best they could. One felt that all hearts were possessed with one and the same thought, wish, and hope,—the hearts of the men who were going slowly up to battle, and those of the people who watched them pass and sent their good wishes with them.

At one station where we stopped a group of girls dressed in white were waiting on the platform under the burning rays of the sun. With simplicity, grace, and charming smiles they distributed chocolate, bread, and fruit to all the men. The good fellows were so touched that tears came to their eyes. One of them, an elderly man with a small grey pointed beard, could not help saying: "But we aren't going to fight, you know. We are only here to take care of the train."

"That doesn't matter. That doesn't matter. Take it all the same. You are soldiers, like the others.... Vive la France! "And all the thirty Territorials, in deep and solemn tones, repeated "Vive la France! "

What a change had come over these men who, people feared, were ripe for revolt, undisciplined, and reckless! What kindness and grace in the women who stay at home and suffer! An old railwayman said to me: "It has been like that, Sir, from the first day of the mobilisation. These girls pass their days and nights at the station. It is really very good of them, for they won't make anything by it." The old working man was right: "They won't make anything by it." And yet I am sure that many soldiers who have passed that station on their way to the Front will keep the same grateful remembrance that I still have. I shall never forget the group of girls in white on the sunny platform of the little station; I shall never forget the simple grace with which they prevailed upon the men to accept the good things they offered and even forced upon them. I thanked them as best I could, but awkwardly enough, trying to interpret the thoughts of all those soldiers. And when the train had started again on its panting course, I felt sorry I had not been more eloquent in my speech; that I had already forgotten the name of the little station, and never thought of asking the names of our benefactresses.

We were now getting near the fighting zone, and I already felt that there was a change in the state of mind of the people. They still called out to us: "Good luck!... Good luck!" But earlier in the day this greeting had been given with smiles and merry gestures; now it was uttered in a serious and solemn tone. At the station gates and the level crossings, the eyes of the women who looked at us were more sad and profound. They fixed themselves upon ours, and seemed to speak to us. And even when their lips did not move their eyes still said "Good luck!... Good luck!"

We saw motor cars rushing along the roads, and could distinguish the armbands on the men's sleeves, and rifles in the cars or lying in the hoods. And yet daily life was going on as usual. There were workers in the fields, tradespeople on the doorsteps of their shops, groups of peasants just outside the hamlets. But yet a peculiar state of mind was evident in each one of these people who were going on with their daily work. And all these accumulated cares, all these stirred imaginations, produced a strange atmosphere which infected everything, seemed to impregnate the air we breathed, and quenched the gaiety of the men in our train. Wattrelot and I were overcome by a kind of religious emotion; we felt as though we were already breathing the air of battle.

At about six o'clock we arrived at the station of L., where the train stopped for a few minutes. The platforms were crowded with Staff officers. A soldier assured me that the chief Headquarters were here. I wanted to question some one and try to get some authoritative information as to what was happening at the Front. It seemed to me that I had a right to know, now that I was on the point of becoming one of the actors in the tragedy in progress a few leagues off. But directly I came up to these officers I felt my assurance fail me. They looked disturbed and anxious. There was none of that merry animation that had reigned in the interior and that I had expected to find everywhere.

And then a strange and ridiculous fear came over me;

the fear of being looked upon as an intruder by these well-informed men who knew everything. I imagined that they would spurn me with scorn, or that I should cause them pain by forcing them to tell me truths people do not like to repeat. It also occurred to me that I was too insignificant a person to confront men so high in office, and that I should appear importunate if I disturbed their reflections. But I was now quite sure that the official announcements had not told us all. Without having heard one word, I felt that things were not going so well as we had hoped, as every day in our little town in the west we tried passionately to divine the truth, devouring the few newspapers that reached us.

A pang shot through me. I now felt alone and lost amongst these men who seemed strangers to me. Crossing the rails, I got back to our train, drawn up at some distance from the platforms. The sun was on the horizon. In the red sky two monoplanes passed over our heads at no great height. The noise of their engines made everybody look up. They were flying north. And I felt a desire to rush upwards and overtake one of them and take my seat close to the pilot, behind the propeller which was spinning round and sending the wind of its giddy speed into his face. I longed to be able to lift myself into the air above the battlefields, and there, suspended in space, try to make out the movements of the clashing nations.

I resolved to have a talk with the engine-driver of a train returning to Paris empty. He told me in a few words that the French army was retreating rapidly, that it had already recrossed the Belgian frontier, and that at that moment it was fighting on French soil. He told me this simply, with a touch of sadness in his voice, shaking his head gently. He added no comments of his own, and I did not feel equal to any reply. Full of foreboding, I returned to my train and Wattrelot. He had heard what the engine-driver had told me, and he said not a word, but looked out into the distance at the fiery sky. We sat down side by side and said nothing.

So we were retreating. Then all our calculations and dreams were shattered. All the fine plans we officers had sketched out together were folly. We were wasting time when, bending over our maps, we foresaw a skilful advance on the heels of Belgium's invaders, followed by a huge victory, dearly bought, perhaps, but one that would upset the German Colossus at a single blow. The whole thing was an illusion. And I thought what a fool I had been. I thought of my regiment. How much of it was there left? How many of those good fellows were lying dead on foreign soil? How many friends should I never see again? For I imagined things to be worse than they really were. I felt absolutely despondent. What my mind conjured up was no longer a retreat in good order but a rout.

The train had begun to move again. The sun had set, and over the horizon there was but a streak of pale yellow sky lighting up the country. I sat down in the open doorway with my legs dangling outside, and as I breathed the first few whiffs of fresh air I felt somewhat relieved. The calm around was such as to make one forget that we were at war. Darkness came on by degrees.

Suddenly my heart began to beat faster, and I rose with a nervous movement. Wattrelot too had started up from the straw he had been lying on. We both exclaimed in one breath: "Cannon!" It was a mere distant growl, hardly audible, and yet it was distinct enough to be a subdued accompaniment to the thousand noises a train makes as it goes along. We could not distinguish the shots, but gradually the dull sound became louder and seemed to be wafted towards us by a gust of air. Then it seemed to be further off again, and almost to die away, and again to get louder. There is no other earthly sound like it. A thunderstorm as it dies away is the only thing that could suggest the impression we felt. It sends a kind of shiver all over the surface of the body. Even our horses felt it. Their three heads were raised uneasily, their eyes shone in the twilight, and they snorted noisily through their dilated nostrils.

Leaning out, I saw the heads of the Territorials thrust out of the windows. They, too, had heard the mysterious and stirring music. No one spoke or joked. Their bodies, stretching out into space, seemed to be asking questions and imploring to know the truth. We came nearer to the sounds of the guns and could now distinguish the shots following one another at short intervals. The air seemed to be shaken, and we might have thought we were but a few paces off.

The train had pulled up sharply in the open country. It was still light enough for us to make out the landscape—meadows covered with long pale grass, bordered by willows and tall poplar trees gently swaying in the evening breeze. In the background a thick wood shut in the view. The railway line curved away to the right and was lost to view in the growing darkness. Now that the train was motionless the impressive voice of the cannon could be heard more distinctly. The long luminous trails of the search-lights passed over the sky at intervals.

Impatient at the delay, I got down and walked along the line to the engine. It had stopped at a level crossing. At the side of the closed barrier, on the doorstep of her hut, with the light shining upon her, sat the wife of the gate-keeper, a child in her arms. She was a young woman, fair and pale. She seemed somewhat uneasy, and yet had no idea of quitting her post. She was talking in a low voice to the engine driver and stoker of our train. I tried to get some information from her. "Mon Dieu, monsieur," she said, "I know nothing, except that the guns have been firing all day long since yesterday, and even at times during the night. The sound comes chiefly from the direction of G. Some soldiers, who went by just now with carts, told me the Prussians got into the town yesterday, but that it was to be retaken to-day; and that there were a great many dead and wounded."

My hopes revived a little. I saw at once in my mind the German attack stopped on the river Oise, our armies recovering, drawing together and driving the enemy back across the frontier. Our engine-driver explained to me that we had come quite close to the terminus, but that we should have to wait some time before we could get in. Other trains had to be unloaded and shunted to make room.

I went back to my van. Night had fallen, and it must have been about nine o'clock. The guns had suddenly ceased firing. Our lantern had burnt itself out, and the rest of our wait was made more tedious by darkness. An empty train passed us, and then silence fell once more upon the spot where we waited anxiously to be allowed to go forward towards our brothers-in-arms. Oh! how I longed to join them, even if it were only in the middle of a bloody and difficult retreat; how I longed to be delivered from my solitude!

At last, at about eleven o'clock, the train set off again without whistling, and very slowly. It went along timidly, so to speak, and as though it was afraid of coming into some unknown region which might be full of mysteries and ambuscades. In the distance I saw some signal lamps waved, and suddenly we stopped. What I then saw astounded me. I had thought we should draw up at a large platform where gangs of men would be waiting, in perfect order, to unload the train, sort out the packages, and pile them up in their appointed places for the carts to take them quietly away.

Instead of this the train stopped at some little distance from a small station standing by itself in the open country. I could make out some buildings, badly lighted, and around them a crowd of shadowy forms moving about. And drawn up alongside of our train were countless vehicles of all sorts and kinds in indescribable disorder, made all the more confusing by the darkness. Some of them were drawn up in some sort of a line. Others tried to edge themselves in and get a vacant place among the entanglement of wheels and horses. The drivers were abusing each other in forcible language. Every now and again there was an outburst of laughter interspersed with oaths.

All this time officials were running down the platform with papers in their hands, trying to read what was chalked on the vans. Enquiries and shouts were heard:

"Where is the bread?"

"Over here."

"No, it's not."

"Where is the officer in charge?"

Matches were struck. The few lighted lanterns there were were snatched from one hand by another. And in spite of all this apparent disorder the work went rapidly forward. Men climbed in through the open doors. Sacks and heavy cases were passed along. Porters, bending under their loads, slipped through the maze of vans and carts to the one they wanted and deposited their burdens.

After giving Wattrelot orders to prevent any one from invading our horse-box I slipped out and went towards the station office to look for the military commissary. I had great difficulty in making my way through the crowd of men who seemed to be rushing to take the train by assault in the darkness. Then I had to avoid breaking my neck in getting across the maze of rails, the signal wires, and the open ditches.

I got to the station. A number of wounded were there lying on the platforms; about a hundred of them, with their clothes torn, and covered with dust. They presented a sad picture. They were, it is true, only slightly wounded; but it cuts one to the heart to see soldiers in that plight, hauled out upon the ground without straw to lie upon or any doctor to attend to them. However, they had all had first-aid dressings. Below the bandages that bound their heads their feverish eyes gleamed in the light of the lanterns. Their bandaged arms were supported by pieces of linen tied behind their necks. Several of them were sitting on baskets, casks and packages of all kinds, and they were talking eagerly. Each man was relating, with plenty of gesticulation, the great deeds he had taken part in or seen. As I passed, I heard scraps of their conversation: "They were in the first line of houses.... Then, old chap, our lieutenant rushed forward.... You should have seen them scuttle...."

I was delighted to see that the moral of those fine fellows didn't seem in the least affected. To hear them you would have thought the Germans had been driven back at all points.

I got a porter to tell me where the military commissary was. He pointed out an Artillery lieutenant, in a cap with a white band, talking to a group of officers. I introduced myself, and asked him if he knew anything about the state of affairs. Like everybody else, he could only give me very vague information. "However," he added, "I can confirm what you have heard about G. The First Corps has just retaken the town, which was defended by the Prussian Guard. It appears that our fellows were wonderful, and that the enemy has suffered enormous losses. However"—the lieutenant's voice trembled slightly, and the shrug of his shoulders betrayed his despair—"I have orders to evacuate the station, with all my men and my papers, so soon as the last train has been unloaded. I am to fall back towards L. How is one to understand what all this means?"

We looked at each other, without a word. Everybody felt dejected and doubtful. Not to understand!... To have to obey without understanding why! It was the first time I had really felt the grandeur of military service. You must have a soul stoutly tempered to carry out an order—no matter what, even if that order seems incomprehensible to you. There must have been in that corner of France, on the edge of that frontier which we had sworn should never be violated—there must have been thousands of officers, thousands of soldiers who would have given their lives rather than yield up one inch of ground. Then why abandon that station? Why say so bluntly, "To-morrow you will have no need to go so far north to bring supplies. We shall come nearer to you; we shall withdraw ..."?

There I was again, allowing my mind to wander and to suffer. I tried to learn by what means I could get some information about my regiment.

"Well, it's very simple," said the Artillery lieutenant, very kindly. "Your commissariat officer will certainly have to come with his convoy to fetch supplies. Try to get hold of him. He will tell you all about it."

I grasped his hand and went off, glad indeed at the thought of seeing my regiment's uniform once more. And Providence seemed to guide me, for I thought I saw the very man I was looking for in the little booking office. But I had some difficulty in recognising him. He looked aged and worn. His beard had grown quite grey. Bending over the sill of the ticket office, he was in the act of spreading the contents of a box of sardines upon a slice of bread. Yes, it was he. How tired and disheartened he looked! I pushed the door open and rushed in:

"Bonjour! Comment va? "

"Ah!... It's you! What have you come here for, my poor fellow? Ah! Things aren't looking very rosy...."

I plied him with questions, and he answered in short incoherent sentences:

"Charleroi? Don't talk of it!... Our men? Grand!... A hecatomb.... Then ... the retreat ... day and night.... The Germans daren't.... Ah! a nice business, isn't it? We're retreating."

He told me where the regiment was, in a huge farm a long way off. He said he could take my canteen in one of his vans. As for me, I should have to manage as best I could next day to join my comrades. It would take some time to get my horses detrained, as the only platform was still being used for the vans not yet unloaded. "Thanks," said I. "Well, it's quite simple. To-morrow I go straight towards the cannon. Good-night." And I went off to finish my sleepless night, lying beside my horses. With my eyes fixed on the chink of the door, I waited, hour after hour, for the daylight....

When dawn broke I had already got Wattrelot and a couple of railwaymen who were still in the station to bring my horse-box up to the platform. The three horses were quickly saddled and ready to start. The freshness of the morning and the joy of feeling firm ground under their feet again made them uncommonly lively. Indeed, Wattrelot came near feeling the effects of their good spirits somewhat uncomfortably as he was getting into the saddle.

At last we started at a quick trot along a white and dusty road which led straight across fields still bathed in shadow. I went first in the direction my friend had vaguely indicated the night before. Wattrelot followed, leading my spare horse. The horses' footsteps resounded strangely in this unknown country where nothing else could be heard. Were we really at war? Everything seemed, on the contrary, to breathe perfect tranquillity. What a change from the feverish bustle of the station the evening before!

We rode through a rich and fertile countryside. The fields

stretched out one after another without end, covering the rounded flanks of the undulating ground with their stubble, dotted with stacks and golden sheaves. A few hedges and some clumps of trees broke the monotony of the landscape. Here and there farms of imposing proportions appeared among the foliage. No shots were to be heard, nor any sound of marching troops. And this made me so uneasy that I began to wonder whether something had not happened during the night to shift the scene of the fighting without my knowledge. But I was about to see something which was to remind me, better than the noise of cannon, that the scene of the strife was not far off.

As the daylight became gradually brighter we distinguished figures moving round some straw-stacks—folks who had collected there to pass the night sheltered as much as possible from the cold and the morning dew. I thought they were soldiers who had lost touch with their regiments and had taken their brief night's rest in the open air. But I soon saw my mistake. As by enchantment, as soon as the first rays of the sun appeared the sleepers got up, and I saw that they were civilians, mostly women and children. They were the unfortunate country-folk who had fled before the barbarian hordes. They had preferred to forsake their homes, to leave them to the invader, rather than fall into his hands. They had fled, carrying with them the most precious things they possessed. They had come away not knowing where they would stop, nor where they could pass the night. And as soon as the twilight came and found them exhausted on the interminable roads, they had dropped down by the stacks grateful for a humble bed of straw. There they had stretched their aching limbs, the mothers had carefully made up little beds for their babies, families had nestled closely together, and often whole villages had gathered in the same fields and around the same stacks.

And when the daylight appeared they had got up hurriedly and the roads were already crowded with mournful pilgrims seeking refuge further and further inland. I must confess that I had not expected to see such a sight. It made my heart ache. I was seized with a fury and longed to be able to rush upon the enemy, drive him back across the frontier, and restore the dwellings forsaken by these poor folks.

What human being, however cold-hearted, could help feeling deep pity at the sight of those poor, weak and inoffensive creatures fleeing before invasion? There were pitiable sights on every hand. A mother pushing a perambulator containing several small children, whilst five or six others were hanging on to her dress or trotting along around her. Poor invalids, dragged, pushed, carried by all possible means, sooner than be left in the hands of the Prussians. Old men helped along by boys; infants carried by old men. And as they passed they all cast a look of distress at the officer who rode quickly by, averting his eyes. I thought I saw a reproach in those glances: they seemed to say to me: "Why haven't you been able to defend us? Why have you let them come into our country? See how we are suffering. Look at our little children, who cannot walk any further. Where are we to go now that, by your fault, we have left the homes of our childhood, and of our fathers and our fathers' fathers? Is that what war is?" I urged on my horse to get them out of my sight and to reach the fighting line as quickly as I could.

Suddenly the report of a gun sounded straight in front of me. Further off a few rifle shots were audible, and then guns again, accompanied by concentrated rifle fire. A kind of shiver passed through my whole body.

My first battle! I was going to take part in my first battle! I felt really mad and intoxicated at the thought of at last realising the dream of my life. But other feelings were mingled with it. I reflected: "What effect will it have upon me? I expect I shall come into the middle of the fight when I get over that ridge. Shall I duck my head when I hear the bullets whistling and the shrapnel bursting around me? I am determined to play the man. I know Wattrelot is close by, trotting behind me. He mustn't see the least symptom of nervousness in me."

The noise of the guns became louder. "By the way!... I wonder what Wattrelot feels like!" I turned to look at him, and found his face a bit pale; but directly he saw me glance at his blue north-country eyes, his face lit up with a broad smile.

"Here we are, sir."

"Yes, Wattrelot, here we are. I'm sure you don't know what fear is!"

"Oh! no, sir."

"That's all right. Forward then! To the guns!"

We passed through a hamlet full of waggons and motors. Some orderlies were loading them up with rations and boxes. On one of these I happened to see the number of my own army corps. "I'm all right then," thought I, and turned to an adjutant of the Army Service Corps, who was superintending the work.

"Do you know where the Staff of the—Corps is?" I asked.

The man shrugged his shoulders to show that he didn't, and that he didn't care. What did it matter to him? His job was to get the goods loaded, forget nothing, and then to go to his appointed post where he would have to wait for further orders to unload his stuff in the evening. He had enough to do. What did anything else matter to him? However, he pointed in a vague manner: "They went over there...."

Off I started again over the wide undulating plain. The

noise of the cannonade became louder and louder, and I now perceived traces of the work of death. At a turning of the road there were a couple of dead horses that had been dragged into the ditch. I cannot say how painful the sight was to me. Apparently a dead horse at the seat of war is a trifle, and no doubt I should very soon see it with indifference. But these were the first I had seen, and I could not help casting a glance of pity at them. Poor beasts! A month before they had been showing off their fine points in the well-kept stables of the artillery barracks. When I saw them their stiffened corpses bore traces of all their sufferings. Their harness had rubbed great sores in their flesh, in more places than one. Their glazed eyes seemed to be still appealing for pity. They had fallen down exhausted, finding it impossible to keep up with their fellows. They had been quickly unharnessed, so as not to block up the road; had been dragged on to the sunburnt grass, and it was there no doubt the death-agony that had already lasted for some hours had come to an end.

We went on, and, in the distance, here and there on the plain, which now stretched before us for miles, we saw more of them. I wondered how it was that so many horses had fallen in so short a time. It was not a month since mobilisation had been ordered, and hardly ten days since operations had begun. What a huge effort then the army must already have made!

But I soon forgot the poor beasts, for we were nearing the scene of the struggle. Behind the shelter of every swell in the ground were ammunition waggons. I went up to one of these and was astonished at what I saw. The limbers, which are always so smart in the barrack-yard, with their grey paint, were covered with a thick coating of dust or of hardened mud. The horses, dirty and thin, seemed ready to drop. Their necks were covered with sores, and they were hanging their heads to eat, but seemed not to have strength enough to take their food. Drivers and non-commissioned officers were sprawling about, sleeping heavily. Their cadaverous faces, beards of a week's growth and drawn features showed even in their sleep how exhausted they were. I could hardly recognise the original colour of their dingy uniforms under the accumulation of stains and dust.

It was now eight o'clock in the morning. The sunshine was beating hot upon the sleepers, but they seemed indifferent to this. They had simply pulled the peaks of their caps over their eyes and were snoring away, with their noses in the air and their mouths open. Beasts and men together formed a group of creatures that seemed utterly depressed and worn out. I could never have believed it possible to sleep under such conditions, with the guns booming unceasingly in all directions.

I went up the nearest ridge and thence got a glimpse of a corner of the battle. I had expected to see a sight similar to that which had delighted us at manoeuvres; troops massed in all the depressions of the ground, battalions advancing in good order along the roads, and mounted men galloping about on the higher ground. But there was nothing of the sort.

In front of me, about 600 yards off, and under cover of the brow of a hill carpeted with russet stubble, I saw two batteries of artillery, firing their guns. I looked intently. The pieces were in perfect line and the gunners at their posts. The shots were fired at regular intervals and with cool deliberation. The gunners took their time, and seemed to be working very casually. I had expected to see them fairly excited: the men running under a hail of shells, teams brought up at a gallop as soon as a few salvoes had been fired, and the guns whirled off at full speed and lined up in battery again some hundreds of yards further off.

On the contrary, these guns seemed to be planted there for good. The limbers, which were massed to the rear under cover of a slope, looked very much like the sections of munitions I had seen just before. The men were sleeping in the shadows of their horses, and the horses were asleep on their feet in their appointed places. The only man standing was a stout-looking adjutant who was walking up and down with his hands in his pockets. With his eyes on the ground he seemed to be counting his steps. And meanwhile, the two batteries went on firing salvoes of four at a time. When one was finished there was a pause of two or three minutes. Then the other battery took it up.

But Wattrelot interrupted my reverie: "Look over there, sir.... Ça barde! "I looked in the direction he was pointing out. And now I no longer felt the uneasy feeling that had come over me at the sight of what was going on here. Above a height that overtopped the hill on which I was, and about 1,500 yards away, the German shells were bursting incessantly. We could distinctly hear the sharp sound of the explosions. In the clear blue of the sky they made little white puffs which vanished gradually and were replaced by others. Their gunners could not have been firing with the same coolness as ours, for the white puffs increased in number. The noise they were making on the spot must have been deafening. From where I was we heard the explosions following one upon another without intermission.

But what was most thrilling was to watch one of our own batteries in action under this avalanche of projectiles. The slope on which it was placed was in shadow still. Against this blue-grey background short flames could be seen flashing for a second at the muzzles of the guns. And the four reports reached us almost at the same moment. The gunners could be seen just as calm under fire as the others here. The German shells, that tried to scatter death among them, ırst too high. They were trying to annihilate this battery, hich was no doubt causing terrible ravages among their ıııen. But the broken fragments fell wide, and our gunners worked their pieces gallantly. This was something that more than made up for my touch of disappointment at first. My hope revived, and I started off at a trot straight in front of me, getting past the ridge, under cover of which the pair of batteries were plying their guns.

No sooner had I gained the further slope than I understood that what I had seen hitherto was only the background of the battle. From this spot a violent rifle fire was heard in every direction. In the meadows were a large number of infantry sections crouching behind every available bit of cover. On the opposite slope long lines of skirmishers were deployed. And dotted about everywhere, above their heads, rose puffs of smoke—white, black, and yellow—the German shells bursting. The noise of them was incessant, and the spot where we were seemed to me very quiet, in spite of the firing of the two batteries close behind us.

Everything was wonderfully coloured by the sunshine. The red trousers of the soldiers, lying in the grass, showed up brightly. The mess-tins on their knapsacks and the smallest metal objects—buttons, bayonet-hilts, belt-buckles—glittered at every movement. On my left, in a dip of ground with a little river running down it, a gay little village seemed to be overflowing with troops. I rode towards it in haste, hoping to find a Staff there which could give me some information.

The streets were, in fact, full of infantry, lying about or sitting along the houses on both sides. In the middle of the main road was a crowd of galloping orderlies, cyclists and motor-cyclists. I felt rather bewildered in all this bustle. However, these people seemed to know where they were going. They were, no doubt, carrying orders or information. And yet I could see no chief officer who appeared to be busying himself about the action or directing anything. Those who were not sleeping were chatting in little groups. The soldiers of different arms were all mixed together, which had, perhaps, a picturesque effect, but was disconcerting.

Suddenly I heard some one call me by my name. I turned round and hesitated a moment before I recognised in an artillery captain with a red beard, a former friend who had been a lieutenant in a horse battery at Lunéville. Yes, it was he. I recognised him by his grey eyes, his hooked nose, and his ringing voice.

"Eh, mon cher! What are you doing here? You look fresh and fit!... What are you looking for? You seem to be at sea."

I explained my position to him, and asked him to tell me what had happened.

"Oh! that would take too long. Your fellows were at Charleroi with us; they had some experiences! But hang it if I know what they are doing with us. We beat them yesterday, my friend. Our men and our guns did wonders. And now there's talk of our retreating further south. I don't understand it all. Ah! we have seen some hot work, and you will make a rough beginning.... Looking for your regiment, are you? I haven't seen it yet to-day. But you see that Staff right over there behind those stacks?... Yes, where those shells are bursting.... That's General T. He can help you; only, you see, he's not exactly in clover. T. has been splendid; always under fire, cheering on his men. They say he wants to get killed so as not to see the retreat...."

I knew General T. well. He commanded a brigade in our garrison town of R. And a kindly chief he was, clear-minded, frank, and plain-spoken. I soon made up my mind to go to him and see what help I could get to enable me to rejoin my regiment. It would be a pleasure, too, to see him again.

I measured the distance with my eye—a kilometre, perhaps. There was no road, and to go across the fields would not be very easy, as there were walls and hedges round the meadows. I took the other way out of the village, and just as Wattrelot and I were leaving it we saw some wounded men arriving. They came slowly, helped along by their comrades, and there were such a number of them that they blocked the road. Those faces tied up with bandages clotted with perspiration, dust, and blood; those coats hanging open; those shirts torn, and showing lint and bandages reddened with blood; those poor bandaged feet that had to be kept off the ground—all this made a painful impression on me. No doubt this was because I was not accustomed to such sights, for others hardly took any notice of it.

"The ambulance! Where is the ambulance?" cried the men who were helping them along.

"At the station," answered some soldiers, hardly looking round; "go straight on, and turn to the left when you get to the market-place."

And the sad procession went its way. I jumped the ditch at the side of the road, and struck across the fields, spurring straight for General T. At that moment the rifle fire became more violent. Some forward movement was certainly beginning, for the infantry sections, that were lying in cover at the bottom of the valley, began to climb up the slope of the ridge on which I was galloping. Suddenly my horse swerved sharply. He had just almost trodden upon a body lying on the other side of the low wall of loose stones that I had just jumped. I drew rein. A sob burst from my lips. Oh! I did not expect to see that so suddenly. A score of corpses lay scattered on that sloping stubble-field. They were Zouaves. They seemed almost to have been placed there deliberately, for the bodies were lying at about an equal distance from one another. They must have fallen there the day before during an attack, and night had come before it had been possible to bury them. Their rifles were still by their side, with the bayonets fixed. The one nearest to us was lying with his face to the ground and was still grasping his weapon. He was a handsome fellow, thin and dark. No wound was visible, but his face was strikingly pale under the red chéchia which had been pulled down over his ears.

I looked at Wattrelot. The good fellow's eyes were filled with tears. "Come!" thought I, "we must not give way like this."

"Wattrelot, my friend, we shall see plenty more. You know, they were brave fellows who have been killed doing their duty. We must not pity them...."

Wattrelot did not answer. I galloped off again towards the big rick by which stood General T.'s Staff. I had already forgotten what I had seen, and my attention was fixed upon that small group of men standing motionless near the top of the ridge. German shells kept bursting over them from time to time. We were now about 100 yards off, so I left Wattrelot and my spare horse hidden behind a shattered hovel and went alone towards the rick.

But just as I was coming up to it I heard a curious hissing noise which lasted about the twentieth part of a second, and, above my head—how high I could not quite tell—vr-ran!... vrran!—two shells exploded with a tremendous noise. I ducked my head instinctively and tried to make myself as small as possible on my horse. A thought passed through my mind like a flash: "Here we are! Why on earth did I come up here? My campaign will have been a short one!" And then this other thought followed: "But I'm not hit! That's all their shells can do! I shan't trouble to duck in future."

And yet I was disagreeably impressed: a soldier who had been holding a horse just before about 30 yards from me ran down the slope, whilst the horse was struck dead and lay in a pool of blood, his body torn open.

But I was now close to the officers composing the Staff of the T. Brigade. They came towards me, supposing, probably, that I was bringing some information or an order. One of them was known to me, an infantry captain who had been in garrison at R. with me. We shook hands, and I explained the object of this unusual visit. He replied:

"Your regiment? You will find it to the left of the Army Corps. It's the regiment that ensures our liaison with the— Corps."

"Well, Captain, it seems our troops are advancing. Things are going well!"

He shrugged his shoulders sharply. His eyes were hard and sombre as he gazed fixedly at the horizon in the direction of the enemy, and then said in an exasperated tone:

"Certainly, they are advancing. See those lines of skirmishers working along there to the right of the village. And those others further off, there where you see those puffs of yellow smoke. But that won't prevent us from beginning our retreating movement at noon. There are express orders. We must move together with the whole army. We shall sleep to-night 20 kilometres from here ... and not in the right direction!"

We looked at one another in silence. I didn't like to ask any further questions, nor to express my disappointment and the angry feeling that was becoming stronger in me. The sight of General T. calmed me at once. It seemed to tell me what my duty was, and to impose silent obedience and firm faith in our chiefs.

Standing alone, 100 yards in advance of his officers, whom he had told to remain concealed behind the enormous stack, the General was observing the struggle. He stood perfectly still, with his back slightly bent and his hands behind him. He had allowed his beard to grow, and it formed a white patch on his slightly tanned face. In front of him, at some little distance, two shells had just burst, falling short. The General had not stirred. He looked like a statue of sadness and of duty. I had thought of going and introducing myself; but I now felt that I was too insignificant a being to intrude myself upon a chief who was watching the advance of his brave soldiers, as a father watches over his children.

I turned and went away, quietly and slowly, with a feeling of oppression.

So I made my way back again, skirting the firing line behind the ridge, often obliged to pull up to allow troops to pass to reinforce the line. Now and then it seemed that the fighting had ceased at the spot I happened to be in, but I soon found myself again in the thick of the artillery and rifle fire. On all the roads I crossed there was a continual stream of wounded men limping along and stretcher-bearers carrying mutilated bodies. The heat had become tropical. It was nearly twelve o'clock. My head began to swim. My shako seemed gradually to get tighter and to press on my temples till they were ready to burst. I thought I should never find my regiment—never....

I came to a small village, and decided to stop and get some food for ourselves and for my horses, as they showed signs of distress. There, too, the streets were full of infantry, but, to my astonishment, none of them belonged to any of the regiments of my Corps. So I supposed I had passed its left wing without knowing it. Bad luck! I rode up the steep alleys, looking for some inn where I could put up, but all the inns were filled with hot, footsore soldiers, who seemed thankful for a moment's rest. They were sitting about wherever there was any shade to be found. With their coats unbuttoned, their neckties undone and shirts open, they were trying to recover their vigour by greedily devouring hunks of bread they had in their wallets, spread with the contents of their preserved meat tins.

At the door of the vicarage, near the pretty little church which could be seen from the surrounding country, I saw an old priest who was distributing bottles of white wine to an eager crowd of troopers. I heard him say in a gentle voice:

"Here, my lads, take what there is. If the Prussians come, I don't want them to find a drop left."

"Merci, ... merci, Monsieur le Curé ."

All at once there was a frightful explosion quite close to us, which made the whole church-square quiver. A German "coal-box" had fallen on to the roof of the church, making an enormous hole in it, out of which came a thick cloud of horrible yellow smoke. A shower of wreckage fell all around us and made a curious noise. The windows of all the houses came clattering down in shivers. In a twinkling the little square in front of the vicarage was empty. A few men who were wounded fled moaning. The rest slung their rifles and went off quickly in a line close under the shelter of the houses. I was left alone face to face with the white-haired priest who still held a bottle of golden wine in his hand. We looked at each other greatly distressed.

"Tenez, Monsieur l'Officier," he said suddenly; "take some more of this. I am going to break all the remaining bottles, so that they shall not drink any of it.... Ah! the savages! Ah! the wretches!... My church!... My poor church!..."

And he went across his little garden quickly, without listening to my thanks. I handed the bottle to Wattrelot, who stuffed it into his wallet with a smile of satisfaction.

But a second "coal-box" soon followed the first. It was certainly not the place to stay in, so I decided to be off and postpone my luncheon until I could find a rather more sheltered dining-room. As I left the village I saw one of our batteries moving briskly away. It was the one that had been in action close to the village, and had probably been the target of the German gunners. It went rapidly down the slope. The drivers brandished their whips and brought them down upon the haunches of their jaded animals. They had to make haste, for the position had become untenable. The German guns were concentrating their fire on the hapless village and the neighbouring ridge. The formidable shells burst in threes. The ground shook. It was evident that very soon nothing would be left there but ruins.

I resumed my wanderings. I saw then that what the captain had told me was true. The retreating movement was beginning to be obvious. Whilst the firing grew more intense along the whole line small parties of infantry marched across the fields in an opposite direction to the one they had taken two hours previously.

So we were beating a retreat. However, I had seen it with my own eyes; not only had we held our ground along the whole line, but at several points our soldiers were making headway. And then suddenly, and without any apparent reason, we had to withdraw. It was enough to make one mad. We had to retreat over the soil of our France and give it up, little by little, to the hordes which followed on our heels.... I had slackened rein, and was allowing my horse to go as he liked over the country strewn with troops. He seemed to understand what was happening, and with his head lowered, as though he did it reluctantly, he slowly followed the direction the immense army was taking. I was seized with a deep feeling of hopelessness. I doubted everything; our men, of whose bravery and tenacity I had just seen proof;

and our leaders, whose courage I knew. My head seemed to be on fire.

But I heard a ringing voice behind me, calling me by my name. I turned, and my sadness gave way to joy as I recognised two light-blue tunics with red collars. I had found the uniform of my regiment! and my hope revived. I felt I was no longer alone, and that we might yet accomplish great things.

In front of a score of our Chasseurs rode two good friends of mine, Lieutenant B. and Lieutenant of Reserve de C. What a pleasure it was to shake their hands, and to see their bronzed faces and dusty garments.

We now went on together, chatting merrily. C. knew the village where the regiment was to be billeted. We went straight for it at a trot. It was there that, at nightfall, I was going to find my chiefs again, my comrades and my men; and I should at last take my part in the fighting. I could not know what the days to follow had in store for me, but I did know that none could be so cruel for me as the day when I went to the Front. I was now in the bosom of my military family, and I looked forward to taking my share of danger at the head of the brave Chasseurs I knew so well. Doubtless I should now know where we were going; why we had to advance, and why to retire.

It seems that moral suffering is less keen when it can be shared with others. I shall never suffer again what I suffered that day.

Chapter 2

The First Charge

September 4th, 1914

Six o'clock in the evening.

The atmosphere was heavy and stifling. The regiment had been formed into two columns, to the right and the left of the high-road from Vauchamps to Montmirail. The men, tired out, their faces black with dust, had hardly dismounted when they threw themselves on the ground and slept in a field of cut corn. The officers chatted together in groups to keep themselves awake. Nights are short when you are on campaign. The bivouac was pitched at midnight and was to be struck at three o'clock in the morning.

And since six o'clock the battle had been raging, for the enemy had engaged our rearguard almost immediately. This had happened each day of that unforgettable retreat, begun at the Sambre and pushed beyond the Marne. Each day we had had to fight. Each day the enemy was repulsed. Each day we were obliged to retire.

Brother-soldiers!—you who came through those painful hours—shall you ever forget them? Shall you ever forget the anguish that wrung your hearts when, as the sun was sinking, you, who had seen so many of your comrades fall, had to give up a further portion of our sweet France; to deliver up some of our lovely hamlets, some of our fields, our orchards, our gardens, some of our vineyards, to the barbarians?...You were ordered to do so. We have learnt, since then, how important such sacrifices were. But, at the time, we did not know ... and doubt came into our minds. We passed through cruel days, and nothing will ever efface the impression of physical and moral prostration that overcame us then.

The regiment was sleeping—tired out.

Alone, calm, phlegmatic, the Colonel kept watch, standing in the middle of the road. With his pipe between his teeth, beneath his ruddy drooping moustache, his cap pulled over his eyes, his arms crossed on his light-blue tunic, he seemed to be the ever-watchful shepherd of that immense flock. At such moments the chief must be able to seem unconscious of the self-abandonment, the disorder and the exhaustion of his men. Human powers have their limits. They had been expended for days without stint. Every moment of cessation from actual fighting had to be a moment of repose. The important thing is that the chief should keep watch. Brave little Chasseurs! sleep in peace; your Colonel is watching over you.

I looked at the men of my troop, on the ground in front of their horses. How could I recognise the smart, brilliantly accoutred horsemen, whose uniforms used to make such a gay note in the old-fashioned streets of the little garrison town?

Under the battered shakoes with their shapeless peaks, the tanned and emaciated faces looked like masks of wax. Youthful faces had been invaded by beards which made them look like those of men of thirty or more. The dust of roads and fields, raised by horses, waggons, and limbers, had settled on them, showing up their wrinkles and getting into eyes, noses, and moustaches.

Their clothes, patched as chance allowed during a halt under some hedge, were enamels of many-coloured pieces. A few more days of such unremitting war, and we should have vied with the glorious tatterdemalions of the armies of

Italy and of the Sambre et Meuse, as Raffet paints them.

With their noses in the air, their mouths open, their eyes half shut, my Chasseurs lay stretched out among the legs of their horses and slept heavily. Poor horses! Poor, pretty creatures, so delicate, so fiery, in their glossy summer coats! They had followed their masters' fortunes. How many of them had already fallen under the Prussian bullets; how many had been left dying of exhaustion or starvation after our terrible rides! They seemed to sleep, absorbed in some miserable dream of nothing but burdens to carry, blows to bear, and wounds to suffer. They were hanging their heads, but had not even the strength to crop the green blades growing here and there among the stalks of corn.

I felt uneasy, wondering whether they would still be equal to an effort for the fight that was always likely and always desired.

Suddenly, from the ridge some 800 yards behind us, coming down like a bolt, I saw a horse, at full gallop. Its rider was gesticulating wildly. Strange to say, though not a word had been said, as though awakened by an electric current, every man had got up and had fixed his astonished eyes on the newcomer. He was an artillery non-commissioned officer; his face was crimson, his hair unkempt, his cap had come off his head and was dangling behind by the chin-strap. With a violent jerk he pulled up his foaming horse for a second: "Where is the Colonel—the Colonel?" With one voice the whole squadron replied: "There, on the road. What's the matter?"

He had already set off again at full speed, had reached the Colonel, and was bending down towards him. Even at that distance we could hear some of his words: "Uhlans ... near the woods, ... our guns, our teams...."

Then it was like a miracle. Without any word of command, without any sign, in a moment the whole regiment was on horseback, sword in hand. The Colonel alone had remained standing. With the greatest calmness he asked the sergeant in an undertone for some information; and the man answered him with emphatic gestures. All eyes were fixed upon the group. Everybody waited breathlessly for the order which was going to be given and repeated by five hundred voices, by five hundred men drunk with joy.

We believed the glorious hour was at last come, which we had been awaiting with so much impatience since the opening of the campaign. The charge! That indescribable thing which is the raison d'être of the trooper, that sublime act which pierces, rends, and crushes by a furious onslaught—wild gallop, with uplifted sword, yelling mouth, and frenzied eyes. The charge! The charge of our great ancestors, of those demi-gods, Murat, Lasalle, Curély, Kellermann and so many others! The charge we had been asking for, with all our hearts, ever since the opening of the campaign, and which had always been denied us!

Ah! that famous German cavalry, that set up its doctrine of pushing the attack to the death, what hatred and what contempt had we conceived for them! We had one desire, and one only—to measure ourselves with them. And every time we had seen their squadrons the result had been either that they had turned and retired in good order behind their lines of infantry, or they had drawn us into some ambuscade under the pitiless fire of their deadly machine-guns.

Were we at last to meet them and measure our swords with their lances?

*****

The regiment moved off in one body behind the Colonel, who, riding a big chestnut horse and as calm as at manoeuvres, led us at a gentle trot skirting the little clumps of trees that dotted the plain. A troop had gone forward in a halo of glittering dust to act as an advance guard.

Our horses seemed to have understood what we were about. Or was it we who had passed on to them the fighting spirit that fired us? I felt behind me the thrill that ran through my men. The first rank could not manage to keep the correct distance, the yard and a half, which ought to separate it from its leader. Even the corporal in the centre allowed his horse to graze the haunches of mine, "Tourne-Toujours," my gallant charger, the fiery thoroughbred which had so often maddened me at the riding schools of the regiment and at manoeuvres, by his savageness and the shaking he gave me. "Tourne-Toujours" gave evident signs of excitement. By his pawing the ground every now and then he, an officer's horse, seemed to resent the close proximity of mere troop horses. And certainly, under ordinary circumstances, I should have fallen foul of the rider imprudent enough to ride close to his heels. But on that occasion I merely laughed in my sleeve, knowing that in a few minutes, when the charge had begun, "Tourne-Toujours" would soon have made them all keep their proper distance, and something more.

I took a pleasure in looking at the faces of the men of the third squadron, whose troops were riding in column abreast of us. Their chins were raised, their eyes wide open, intent, under the shade of their cap-peaks, upon the slightest irregularities of the ground ahead. Their hands grasped their sword-hilts tightly. Major B., leaning well forward, and riding between the two squadrons, was practising some furious cutting-strokes. What a grand fight it was going to be! How we should rejoice to see the curved sabres of our comrades rising against the clear sky to slash down upon the leather schapskas of our foe! We waited for the word that was to let loose the pent-up energy of all those tense muscles.

A trooper came back from the advance guard at full speed, and brought up his horse with the spur beside the

Colonel. He reported in short sentences, which we could not hear. The Colonel turned towards our Captain, who was behind him, leaning forward over his horse, all attention, with his sword lowered, receiving the orders given in an undertone. We only heard the last sentence: "I shall support you with the rest of the regiment."

"Thank Heaven!" thought I; "it is we; it is our dear squadron that is to have the honour of attacking first." Every man pulled himself together. Every man felt conscious of all the glory in store for us. Every man prepared to perform exploits which, we felt sure, would astonish the rest of the regiment, of the army, and of France. Forward! Forward! Forward!

The troops had already ridden past the Colonel at an easy gallop, and we suddenly found ourselves strangely isolated in that vast tract of country which, a few minutes before, we had passed over in a body. There was a succession of yellow or green fields, with here and there some leafy thicket. On our left, surrounded by orchards, rose the grey and massive buildings of the farm of Bel-Air. In front of us, some few hundred yards off, there was a dark line of wood, the lower part of which was hidden from us by a slight rise in the ground.

Hardly had the first troop reached the top of the brow when some shots were fired at us. We at once understood. Again we were to be deprived of the pleasure of measuring ourselves with their Uhlans at close quarters. We saw distinctly on the edge of the wood, kneeling and ready to fire, some fifty sharp-shooters in grey uniform and round caps without peaks. We recognised them easily.

It was one of their cyclist detachments that had slipped into the wood and had been quietly waiting for us with rifles levelled. As usual, their cavalry had retired under cover of their line.

What did it matter to us? The wood was not thick enough to prevent our horses from getting through, and the temptation to let the fellows have a taste of our steel was too strong. I rejoiced at the thought of seeing their heavy boots scuttle away through the trees. I resolved to have a thrust at the skirts of their tunics, to help them on a bit.

The Captain understood the general feeling. "Form up!" he cried.

In a twinkling a moving wall had been formed, to the music of merrily clinking stirrups and scabbards and jangling metal; and the gallop towards the wood began.

Just at that moment its skirts were outlined by a circle of fire, and a violent fusillade rang out. Bullets whistled in all directions, and behind me I heard the heavy sound of men and horses falling on the hard ground. In my troop a horse without a rider broke away and came galloping towards me. What did it matter? Forward! Forward!

We were about 200 yards off. We spurred our horses and got into our stride.

Suddenly a horrible fear took the place of the martial joy that had urged us to the fight. We were all struck by the same discouragement, the same feeling of impotence, the same conviction of the uselessness of our sacrifice. We had just realised that the edge of the wood was surrounded with wire, and that it was behind this impassable barrier that the Prussians were calmly firing at us as at a target. What was to be done? How could we get at them and avenge our fellows who had fallen? For one second a feeling of horror and impotent rage passed, like a deep wave, over the squadron. The bullets whistled past us.

But the Captain adopted the wisest course. He saw that retreat was necessary. He had, behind him, more than a hundred human lives, and felt they must be saved for better and more useful sacrifices. With a voice that rose above the noise of the firing, he shouted: "Follow me, in open order!" And he spurred in an oblique direction towards the nearest depression in the ground. But the movement was badly carried out. The men, disheartened, instead of spreading out like a flight of sparrows, rushed off in so compact a body that some more horses were knocked over by the Prussian bullets. How long those few seconds seemed to us! I wondered by what sort of miracle it was that we did not lose more men. But what an uncanny tune the innumerable bullets made in our ears as they pursued us like angry bees! At last we got under cover. Following a gully, the squadron reached a little wood, behind which it was able to re-form. The sweating horses snorted loudly. The men, sullen-mouthed and dejected, fell in without a word and dressed the line.

In the fading light the roll was called by a non-commissioned officer in a subdued voice, whilst I looked on distressfully at the sad results of the useless charge. And yet our losses were not great—three troopers only, slightly wounded, who, far from grumbling at their mishap, seemed proud of the blood that stained their tunics and their hands. The men whose horses had fallen had already come up jogging heavily over the field of lucerne that stretched out before us. One man alone was absent; Paquin, a good little fellow, energetic and well disciplined, whose good humour I found especially attractive both under fire and in camp. But he would come in, no doubt. Cahard, his bed-fellow, told me that his horse had stumbled and thrown him. He thought he had even seen him get up again directly the charge had passed.

"Mon Lieutenant, ... mon Lieutenant, your horse is wounded."

I had dismounted in a moment, and tears came to my eyes. I had forgotten the anger and impatience that

"Tourne-Toujours'" savage temper had so often caused me. What had they done to my brave and noble companion-in-arms? A bullet had struck him inside the left thigh and, penetrating it, had made a horrible wound, as large as my hand, from which the blood was streaming all down his leg. Two other bullets had hit him, one in the flank, the other in the loins, leaving two small red holes. The noble animal had brought me back safely, and then, as he stood still on his four trembling legs, his neck raised, his nostrils dilated, his ears pricked, he fixed his eyes on the distance and seemed to look approaching death in the face. Poor 'Tourne-Toujours,' you could not divine the pain I felt as I patted you, as gently as I should touch a little suffering child!

But I had to shake off the sadness that wrung my heart. The day was gradually sinking, and Paquin had not come in. Two of the men quickly put my saddle on the horse of one of the wounded troopers. Whilst Surgeon-Major P., in the growing dusk, attended to the seriously wounded men stretched on the grass, I made up my mind to go out and see whether my little Chasseur was not still lying out on the scene of the charge.

"Cahard, Finet, Mouniette, Vallée, I want you."

At a gentle trot we sallied out from the cover of the wood. My four men, dispersed at wide intervals to my right and left, stood up in their stirrups from time to time to get a better view.

The guns were silent. Now and again one or two isolated shots were heard. Night had almost fallen. On the horizon a long reddish streak of light still gave a feeble glow. Everything was becoming blurred and mysterious. In front of us stretched the disquieting mass of the wood that so lately had rained death on us. Above our heads flocks of black birds were wheeling and croaking.

"Paquin!... Paquin!... Paquin!..."

My Chasseurs shouted their comrade's name; but no voice answered. We were certainly on the ground the squadron had ridden over. Every now and then we came across the body of a horse, marking our mournful course. A poor mare with a broken leg neighed feebly, as if appealing for help to her stable-companions.

"Paquin!... Paquin!... Paquin!..."

No response. We had to turn back and rejoin the others. War has many of those moments of pain when we have to control our feelings—forget those we love, those who are suffering, those who are dying—and think of nothing but our regiment, our squadron, our troop. Paquin's name would be marked on the roll as "missing"—a solemn word which means so many things, a word that leaves a little hope, but gives rise to so many fears.

Over the fields, under a brilliant moon, the squadron retired in silence. Those who have served in war know that solemn moment when, after a day's fighting, each corps arrives at its appointed place of rest. It is the moment when in normal life nature falls asleep in the peace of evening. It is the moment when in villages and farms lights appear in the lower windows, behind which the family is seated around the steaming soup-tureen after the day's work.

It is some time now since we have tasted the exquisite peace of those moments. Instead, we have grown used to hearing over the wide country a monotonous and barbarous uproar caused by the thousands of cannon, limbers, vans, and vehicles of every kind which are the very life of an army. All these things rumble along methodically in the dark, clanking and creaking, towards a goal invisible and yet sure. Above this huge chaos voices rise in various keys: soldiers astray asking their road; van-drivers urging on their foot-sore teams; words of command given by leaders striving, in the dark, to prevent confusion among their units.

This is the reverse of the shield of battle, the moment when we feel weariness of mind and body and the infinite sadness of remembering those who are no more....

Away in the distance two villages were in flames, luridly lighting up some corners of the scene. That evening seemed to me sadder and more distressing than ever....

Chapter 3
Reconnoitring Courgivault
September 5th, 1914

The provisional brigade which had just been formed, with our regiment and the Chasseurs d'Afrique (African Light Cavalry), was paraded at dawn by our Colonel, who had taken command of it. The united regiments had been formed up under cover of a line of ridges, on the summit of which the watchful scouts stood out against the sky, looking north. The sun was already shining on the motley picture formed by the light uniforms of the dismounted troopers and the motionless rows of horses. They were all half asleep still.

The Colonel had drawn up the officers of the brigade in front of the squadrons. He held a paper in his hand and read it to us in a resonant voice, full of unfamiliar vibrations. On hearing the first few sentences we drew closer around him as by instinct. We could not believe our ears. It was the first time we had heard anything like it since the outbreak of the war.

When he had finished we were all amazed. Had we not been told the day before—when, together with the—Corps, we crossed the Grand Morin closely pressed by the enemy's advance guard—had we not been told that we were going to retire to the Seine? And now in a few noble, simple words the Commander-in-Chief told us that the trials of that hideous retreat were over, and that the day had come to take the offensive. He asked us all to do our duty to the death and promised us victory.

We returned to our squadrons in animated groups. Our delight was quickly communicated to the troops, who understood at once. The men exchanged jests and promises of fabulous exploits. They had already forgotten the fatigues of the fortnight's retreat. What did they care if their horses could hardly carry them further, and if many of them would be incapable of galloping?

What did it matter?

My fellow-officers and I were already making wonderful plans. Those of d'A., who had just finished his course of instruction as lieutenant at Saumur with honours, comprised vast movements of complicated strategy. They culminated in a prodigious but inevitable envelopment of the German armies, De F., more prosaic than the other, dreamt of Pantagruelian repasts liberally furnished with Rhine wines. O., a sub-lieutenant, just fresh from the Military College—which he had left with a No. 1, mind you—seemed like a young colt broken loose; his delight knew no bounds. As for our captain, Captain de la N., our kind and sympathetic chief, he was transfigured. The horrors of the retreat had affected him painfully, but the few lines that had been read to us had sufficed to restore all his joyous ardour.

"Captain, the Colonel wants an officer."

"Hurrah!" It was my turn for duty.... Just a few words of congratulation, some hands stretched out to me, and I went, leaving a general feeling of envy behind me. Here was I in the presence of the Colonel, who, with a map in his hand and surrounded by the superior officers, explained in a few short sentences what he required of me.

"Take the direction of Courgivault. Reconnoitre and find out whether the village is occupied. You will report to me on the road which leads straight from here to the village. The brigade will follow you in an hour by the same road. I am sending two other parties towards such and such villages."

And a few minutes afterwards I was on the road to Courgivault.

I chose from my troop a corporal and four reliable fellows who had already given a good account of themselves. In advance I sent Vercherin, as scout, well mounted on his horse "Cabri," whose powerful haunches stood out above the tall oats. I had full confidence in his vigilance and his shrewdness. I knew his clear blue eyes, and that, if there were anything to be seen, he would see it better than any one else. I knew also that I should have no need to spur his zeal.

On either side of me Corporal Madelaine, Finet, a sapper, Lemaître, and my faithful orderly, Wattrelot, rode along in silence in extended order at a considerable distance from one another. We had learnt by experience since the beginning of the campaign. We were on our guard now against Prussian bullets. We knew what ravages they made directly our troopers were imprudent enough to cluster together. Thus we ran fewer chances of being taken by surprise.

The weather was splendid. How delightful, thought I, would it have been to walk over the fields, on a morning like this, with a gun under my arm, behind a good dog, in quest of partridges or a hare. But I had other game in view—no doubt more dangerous, but how much more exciting!

The air was wonderfully clear, without the least trace of mist. The smallest detail of hedge and ditch could be easily distinguished. Our lungs breathed freely. We foresaw that the heat would be oppressive in a few hours' time, but the fresh air of the night still lingered, and bright pearls of dew still lay on the lucerne and stubble. What a joy to be alive in such delicious surroundings, with the hope of victory in one's heart!

I fancy that those who have not been in this war will not be able to understand me, for I have not the skill to explain clearly what I feel by means of written words. A more practised pen than mine is needed for such a task, a mind more accustomed to analyse feelings.

I seem to have within me the inspiration of a strange power that makes me light as air, and inclined to talk aloud to myself. And if I wanted to speak I certainly should not find the words I wanted. Perhaps it is that I simply want to shout, to cry "Hurrah!" again and again. It must be that, for I find myself clenching my teeth instinctively to prevent myself from giving way to such an untimely outburst.

Nevertheless, it would be a relief to be able to shout at the top of my voice and sing hymns of glory confronting the enemy. I should like to hear the whole army following my example behind me, to hear all the bands and all the trumpets accompanying our advance with those matchless war-songs which thrill the soul and bring tears to the eyes.

Here I was, on the contrary, in conditions of absolute calm, of the most impressive silence conceivable. Until that day the country, at that hour of the day, had echoed with the innumerable noises made by an army in retreat. Thousands of cannon, limbers, and convoys had been passing along all the roads and all practicable by-ways monotonously and ceaselessly. Often, too, the first shots exchanged by the cavalry scouts of both the hostile armies could be heard.

We heard nothing that day. In front nothing stirred: the country seemed deserted; the fields forsaken. Not a living creature showed itself.

Behind us, too, there was complete silence. But I knew that an entire army was there, waiting for us to send information, before advancing to the fight. That information would direct its blows.... I knew my brigade was behind that rise in the ground, and that all, officers and troopers alike, were impatient to rush upon my tracks to the attack. I knew that behind them, lying by sections in the ploughland, thousands and thousands of infantrymen had their eyes fixed in the direction I was taking, and that hundreds and hundreds of guns were ready to pour out death. But that disciplined multitude was silent and, as it were, holding its breath, waiting for the order that was to hurl it forward. I felt in excellent spirits.

It was upon me, and upon a few comrades, that the confidence of so many soldiers rested. It was to be by our directions that the regiments were to rush forward, some here, some there, carrying death and receiving death with, for the first time, the certainty of conquering; since for the first time the Commander-in-Chief had said that conquer they must. And not for an instant had I any fear of not being equal to my task. On the contrary, it seemed to me that I had been destined from all eternity to command this first offensive reconnaissance of the campaign in France.... I felt my men's hearts beating close to mine and in unison with mine.

I had consulted my map before breaking into a trot, and had noticed that the road leading to Courgivault passed through two woods, not very deep, but of considerable extent. I soon came in sight of one of them, at about 500 yards distance, below a ridge which we had just passed. I called out to Vercherin, who had begun to spur his horse towards the wood, to stop. I knew that numbers of men had fallen by having acted in this way—a way we have at manoeuvres, when the enemy are our comrades with white badges on their caps, and when harmless blank cartridges are used instead of bullets. We had very soon learnt from the Germans themselves the way to reconnoitre a wood or a village, and also how they must be held.

How much more dashing it would have been, more in

the light cavalry style, to ride full gallop, brandishing my sword, with my five little Chasseurs into the nearest copse! But I knew then that if it were occupied by the enemy their men would be lying down, one with the soil, using the trees and bushes as cover, till the last moment. Then not one of us would have come out alive.

We were reduced to employing against them their own tactics of mounted infantry. The good old times of hussar charges are past—gone, together with plumes, pelisses waving in the wind, Hungarian braiding, and sabretaches. It would be senseless to continue to be a horseman in order to fight men who are no longer cavalrymen and do not wish to be so. We should fight at a disadvantage, and since the opening of the campaign too many brave soldiers have paid with their lives for their delight in epic fights à la Lasalle.

I searched the edge of the wood carefully with my field-glasses. Before entering it I wanted to be quite sure whether any movement could be discovered, whether any of the brushwood showed signs of being drawn aside by sharpshooters too eager for a shot. My men were on the watch, crouching in attitudes that would have pleased Neuville, their carbines ready, looking with all their eyes and listening with all their ears. Nothing! I called Vercherin with a low whistle. The silence was such that he heard it. He understood the sign I made him, and, holding his carbine high, he went slowly towards the wood and got into it quickly by the road.

My heart beat for a moment when I saw my scout getting near the thick border-line of trees; but now I breathed again. We went in after him, each one by a different opening, and we passed through it as quickly as the horses' legs and the difficulties of the ground would allow. On arriving at the further side I was glad to see my four companions emerging, almost at the same moment, from the thick woody tangle. I could see their grave and confident faces turned towards me. On the ridge in front of us, near a solitary tree, stood Vercherin, clear against the sky and motionless.

We had soon rejoined him, and from this height we saw on the next hill the second wood which hid the village of Courgivault from our view, about a kilometre further off. I feared very much that this second barrier might be used by the enemy as a formidable line of defence, and on that account I ordered the approach to be made with still greater precautions than before. But, as in the first case, we found it empty, and passed through without let or hindrance.

I expected to see Courgivault at once, but a rise in the ground hid it still. I took advantage of this natural cover for getting my men forward without risking a shot. Then, still preceded by Vercherin, we debouched on the plateau on which the village stood.

Those who have found themselves in a similar situation know by experience the sudden emotion that is felt when one sees a few hundred yards off the objective of one's mission, the decisive point one has to reach, cost what it may; the point where one is almost sure to find the enemy in hiding, where one has a suspicion that he sees one, is watching one, silently following all one's movements, and only waiting for the opportunity of picking one off by an unerring shot.

I stopped my men for a moment. Surrounded by green meadows and stubble-fields dotted with apple-trees, lay the grey outskirts of the village It was a very ordinary collection of houses, some of them big farms, others humble cottages. The tiled roofs formed a reddish mass, and above them rose the squat church tower. With my glasses I could distinguish the clock-dial, and could see the time—a quarter past six.

But this clock seemed to be the only thing in the village with any life in it. I looked in vain into the gardens and orchards, which formed a belt of flowers and foliage, for signs of the peaceful animation of country life. And yet it was the time of day when one usually sees housewives coming out of the cowsheds, with their sleeves tucked up and their feet in clogs, carrying pails full of fresh milk—the time when the heavy carts and reaping machines lumber slowly along the brown roads on their way to the day's work. Was it the war that had driven away all those poor village folk, or was it the rough fist of the Teuton that kept them prisoners locked up in their cellars and threatened with revolvers?

And yet, from where I stood, nothing could lead me to suppose that the village was occupied by the enemy. I could not distinguish any work of defence. There did not seem to be any barricade protecting the entrance. No sentinel was visible at the corners of the stacks or under the trees.

To the south of the village, pointing in our direction, the imposing bulk of a large farm protruded, like the prow of a ship. It seemed to form an advanced bastion of a fortress, represented by Courgivault. Its walls were high and white. At the end a strong round tower was planted, roofed with slates; and this enhanced the likeness to a miniature donjon. The road we had followed, winding between the fields, passed, so far as we could judge, in front of its principal entrance. Opposite this entrance there was apparently another road at right angles to the first, its direction marked by a line of trees which bordered it. Along this road, separated by short intervals, a dozen big stacks had the appearance of a threatening line of battle facing us, so as to bar our approach to the village.

All these things were steeped in the same atmosphere of silence, which certainly had a more tragic effect than the din of battle. I was impressed with the idea that the two armies had withdrawn in opposite directions, and that we were left behind, forgotten, at 100 kilometres distance from both of them.

But we had to come to the point. At a sign from me Vercherin reached the first tree of a long row of poplars. The row started from the farm and bordered the road we were following up to about 100 yards from the outer wall. By slipping along from one tree to another he would be able to get near in comparative safety. Suddenly I saw him stop quickly and, standing up in his stirrups, look straight ahead towards the stacks.

There was no need for him to make any sign to me. I understood that he saw something, and I galloped up to him at once. He was as calm as usual, only his blue eyes were a little more dilated, and he spoke more rapidly, with an accent I had not heard before.

"Mon Lieutenant, ... there behind that stack, it seemed to me ... I thought I saw a head rise above the grass...."

I looked in the direction he pointed to with his carbine, which he held at arm's length. I saw nothing but the silent and peaceful village; I had the same impression of a hateful and depressing void. And, strange to say, our two horses, whose reins had been hanging loose on their necks, appeared to be suddenly seized with a simultaneous terror, and both at once turned right round. I managed to bring mine back by applying the spur, and while Vercherin, who was carried further, came back slowly, I used my glasses again, to make a closer inspection of all the points of the village.

Then, at the very moment that I was putting the glasses to my eyes, I saw, at less than 100 yards distance, a whole line of sharpshooters, dressed in grey, rise quickly in front of me. For one short moment a terrible pang shot through us. How many were there? Perhaps 300. And almost at the same time a formidable volley of rifle shots rang out. They had been watching us for a long time. Lying in the grass that lined the road leading to the farm or else behind the stacks, with the admirable discipline which makes them so formidable, they had carried out their orders. Not one of them had shown himself. The Hauptmann (captain) alone, no doubt, put up his head from time to time in order to judge the favourable moment for ordering them to fire. It was he, no doubt, very fortunately for us, who had been perceived by Vercherin just for one moment. If it had not been for the prudence which we had gained by experience not one of us would have escaped. Fortunately every one of my men had kept the place exactly that I had assigned him. Not one of them flinched under the storm. And yet, Heaven knows what sinister music the bullets played around our ears! We had to be off.

I made a sign which was quickly understood. We all turned and galloped off towards the little depression we had emerged from just before. The bullets accompanied us with their hateful hissing, which made us duck our heads instinctively. But inwardly I rejoiced at their eagerness to lay us low, for in their hurry they aimed badly.

We had almost reached our shelter when I suddenly saw to the right of me "Ramier," Lemaître's horse, fall like a log. As I was trying to stop my mare, who showed an immoderate desire to put herself out of danger, I saw both horse and rider struggling for a moment on the ground, forming a confused mixture of hoofs in the air and waving arms. Then "Ramier" got up and set off alone, neighing sadly, and with a limping trot that did not look very promising.

But Lemaître was already on his legs, putting his crushed shako straight on his head. A bit stunned, he seemed to collect his ideas for an instant, and then I saw his good-natured ruddy face turned towards me. It lit up with a broad grin.

"Any damage, old fellow?" I asked.

"Nothing broken, sir."

"Hurry up, then."

And there was Lemaître, striding along with his short legs and heavy boots, jumping ditches and banks with a nimbleness of which I declare I should not have thought him capable. It is curious to note the agility the report of a rifle volley lends to the legs of a dismounted trooper. Lemaître came in to the shelter in the valley as soon as I did; and almost at the same time Finet, the sapper, brought in his old road-companion "Ramier," which he had been able to catch. It was painful to see the poor animal; his lameness had already become more marked. He could only get along with great difficulty, and his eyes showed he was in pain.

I glanced hurriedly at the spot where the bullet had struck him. The small hole could hardly be seen against the brown skin, just at the point of the left buttock.

"Just wait here for us; I shall be back in a moment."

I wanted to see if to the east of the village I could note anything interesting, and I turned round towards my other troopers, whose horses were panting behind us. I was horrified to see Corporal Madelaine's face streaming with blood.

"It is nothing, sir ...; it passed in front of my nose."

He wiped his face with the back of his hand. It had indeed been grazed by a bullet. One half-inch more, and the good fellow's nose would have been carried off. Fortunately the skin was hardly broken. Madelaine went on:

"It's nothing; ... but my mare...."

He had dismounted, and with a look of distress showed me his horse's blood-stained thigh. "Attraction" was the name of his pretty and delicate little grey mare, which he loved and cared for passionately. A bullet had pierced her thigh right through, and the blood had flowed down her leg. I calmed him by saying, "Come, come; it will be nothing. Go on foot behind that wood, and get quietly under cover with Lemaître. I will soon come and join you."

And I went off with Vercherin, Finet, and Wattrelot. I tried to get round to the right of Courgivault. But now that the first shots had been fired we were not allowed to come nearer. As soon as we appeared a violent fusillade burst from the outskirts of the village, which forced us to beat a rapid retreat. There was no longer any doubt about it; Courgivault was occupied, and occupied in strength.

Under the shelter of a bank I quickly dismounted, and Wattrelot took my horse's bridle. Whilst I knelt on one knee and on the other wrote my report for the Colonel, Vercherin and Finet, at an interval of 100 yards, kept a good look-out on the ridge for the enemy's movements. I handed my message to Wattrelot:

"Take this to the Colonel, and quickly. I will wait here for the brigade."

I then rode slowly to the corner of the wood, where Madelaine and Lemaître were posted, whilst Wattrelot went off at a trot across the stubble. But a sad sight was awaiting me.

Lemaître was standing in great grief over poor "Ramier," lying inert on the ground and struggling feebly with death. His eyes were already dull and his legs convulsed. Every now and then he shuddered violently.

I looked at Lemaître, who felt as if he were losing his best friend. And, indeed, is not our horse our best friend when we are campaigning—the friend that serves us well to the very last, that saves us time and again from death, and carries us until he can carry us no longer? I dismounted and threw the reins to Lemaître:

"Don't grieve, my good fellow; it is a fine end for your 'Ramier.' He might, like so many others, have died worn out with work or suffering under some hedgerow. He has a soldier's death. All we can do is to cut short his sufferings and send him quickly to rejoin his many good comrades in the paradise of noble animals. For they have their paradise, I am sure."

But Lemaître hardly seemed convinced. He shook his head sadly, and said:

"Oh, mon Lieutenant ! I shall never be able to replace him. Such a good animal! such a fine creature! He jumped so well.... And his coat was always so beautiful; he was so sleek and so easy to keep.... No, I shall never find another like him."

"Oh! yes, you will."

However, I must confess my hand trembled as I drew my revolver. One horse the less in a troop is somewhat the same as one child the less in a family. And, besides, it means one trooper unmounted and the loss of a sword in battle. Lemaître was right. "Ramier" was a good old servant, one of the kind that never goes lame, can feed on anything or on nothing, and never hurts anybody. It was hard to put an end to him; but since he was done for....

I put the muzzle of my revolver into his ear. I did not wish him to feel the cold metal; but his whole body shuddered, and his eye, lighting up for a moment, seemed to reproach me. Paff! A short, sharp report, and "Ramier" quivered for a moment. Then his sufferings ceased, and his stiffening carcase added one more to the many that strewed the country.

Whilst Lemaître slung his heavy package on his shoulders and went off to return to the regiment with Corporal Madelaine, who was leading "Attraction," I went back to my observation post, not far from Finet and Vercherin. Silence and gloom still hung over Courgivault.

Suddenly, behind me, coming out of the wood, I saw a cavalry troop in extended order, riding in our direction.

They were Chasseurs d'Afrique . I recognised them by the large numbers of white horses, which made light patches upon the dark green of the thicket, and almost at the same moment a dull report resounded in the distance. A curious humming noise was heard above our heads, and a shell fell and burst at the foot of the stacks in the possession of the Prussian infantry. It came from one of our batteries of 75-millimetre guns, which was already getting the range of Courgivault.

My message had reached the Colonel. The battle of the Marne had begun.

* * * * *

Under a superbly clear sky, lit up by myriads of stars, the brigade, in a high state of delight, crossed the battlefield on returning to camp. Above our heads the last shells sent by the enemy were bursting in bouquets of fire. We paid no attention to them. Meeting some battalions of infantry on their way to reinforce the line, we were asked for news, and shouted: "Courgivault, Montceau ... taken, lost, then retaken with the bayonet by the brave infantry of the M. Division. Enemy's regiments annihilated by our artillery, which has done magnificently...."

Little by little the firing died away along the whole line. Fires, started by the shells, lit up the battlefield on every side, like torches set ablaze for our glory. All hearts were filled with joy. It hovered over the blood-stained country, from which arose a kind of intoxication that took possession of our souls.

How splendid is the evening of a first victory!

Chapter 4
The Jaulgonne Affair
September 9th, 1914

At about eight o'clock in the evening, our advanced scouts entered Montigny-les-Condé at the moment when the last dragoons of the Prussian Guard were leaving it at full speed. Our pursuit was stopped by the night, which was very dark. Large threatening clouds were moving across the sky, making it impossible to see ten paces ahead. Whilst the captains were hastily posting guards all round the village, whilst the lieutenants were erecting barricades at all the outlets and setting sentries over them, the quartermasters had all the barns and stables thrown open. With the help of the inhabitants they portioned out, as well as they could, the insufficient accommodation among the men and the horses of the squadrons. In each troop camp fires were lighted under shelter of the walls so that the enemy should not see them.

What a dinner we had that evening! It was in a large room with a low open roof supported by small beams. The walls were smoke-blackened and dirty. On a chest placed near the door I can see still a big pile of ration loaves, thrown together anyhow; and leaning over the hearth of the large fireplace, lit up by the wood fire, was an unknown man who was stirring something in a pot. Round the large table a score of hungry and jaded but merry officers were fraternally sharing some pieces of meat which the man took out of the pot.

The Captain and I ate out of the same plate and drank out of the same metal cup, for crockery was scarce. The poor woman of the house ran round the table, consumed by her eagerness to make everybody comfortable. And in the farthest corner, away from the light, a very old peasant, with a dazed look and haggard eyes, was watching the unexpected scene. The company heartily cheered Captain C. for his cleverness in finding and bringing to light, from some nook or other, a large pitcher of rough wine.

For three days we had been pursuing and fighting the German army, and we were tired out; but we had not felt it until the evening on stopping to give our poor horses a little rest. Before the last mouthful had been swallowed several of us were already snoring with their heads on their arms upon the table.

The rest were talking about the situation. The enemy was retreating rapidly on the Marne. He must have crossed it now, leaving as cover for his retreat the division of the Cavalry of the Guard which our brigade had been fighting unceasingly ever since the battle of September 6. Would they have time to blow up all the bridges behind them? Should we be obliged to wait until our sappers had built new ones before we could resume our pursuit?

We were particularly anxious about two fine officers that our Colonel had just sent out that night on a reconnaissance—F., of the Chasseurs d'Afrique, and my old friend O., of our squadron. We wondered anxiously whether they would be able to perform their task—to get at all costs as far as the Marne, and let us know by dawn whether the river could be crossed either at Mont Saint Père, Jaulgonne, Passy-sur-Marne, or Dormans. Nothing could have been more hazardous than these expeditions, made on a dark night across a district still occupied by the enemy.

The night was short. Before day dawned the horses were

saddled and the men ready to mount. And as soon as the first rays of morning filtered through, my squadron, which had been told off as advance guard of the brigade, rapidly descended the steep slopes which commanded the small town of Condé. A.'s troop led. My business was to reconnoitre the eastern part of the town with mine, whilst F., with his troop, was to see to the western quarters.

With sabres drawn, our Chasseurs distributed themselves briskly, by squads, through the streets of the old city. The horses' hoofs resounded cheerily on the paved streets between the old grey houses. The inhabitants ventured out upon their doorsteps, in spite of the early hour, with some hesitation at first, but glad indeed when they saw our light-blue uniforms; they cheered, crying: "They are gone!... they are gone!" But some old folk replied more calmly to my questions: " Monsieur l'Officier, have a care. They were here an hour ago with a large number of horses and guns. There was even a general, with his whole staff, lodged at the great house up there.... We would not swear that some of them are not there still."

I collected my troop, and then went quickly to the château which stood at the northern entrance of Condé. It was rather a fine building, but I had not time to notice its architectural style. Haste was necessary, for the brigade behind me was due to arrive. As far as I remember, the château formed a harmonious whole, and the different parts of it showed up cheerfully against the dark foliage of the park, which was still glittering after the night's rain. The building was in the form of a horseshoe, and in the centre there was a kind of courtyard bordered by two rows of orange trees in tubs.

I at once posted two guards, one on the road to provide against any surprise and the other at the park entrance to prevent egress, in case any fugitive should attempt to pass.

Then, with the rest of my men, I rode through the large gilded iron gates at a trot. In the avenue which led to the house two men were standing motionless. One of them, dressed in black and clean-shaven, appeared to be some old servant of the family, the other must have been one of the gardeners. Their pale faces and red eyes showed that they had had little sleep that night.

"Well, my friend," said I to one of them, "is there anybody left at your place?"

"Sir," he answered, "I couldn't tell you; for I have not set foot in the house since they left it. What I do know is that they feasted all night and got horribly drunk. They have drunk the whole cellar dry, and I shouldn't be surprised if some of them are still under the table."

But when I asked him to come in with me, to act as guide for our visit, he refused with a look of horror. He trembled all over at the thought of seeing perchance one of the guests who had been forced upon him. As there was no time to be lost, I told my men to dismount at once, and gave orders to one corporal to search the right wing of the building, to another to reconnoitre the left wing. I myself undertook to see about the central block with the rest of my troop. We had to make haste, so I instructed my subordinates to go quickly through the different rooms and not to inspect them in detail.

The entrance door was wide open. Taking my revolver in my hand, I entered the hall, which was in indescribable disorder. Orderlies had evidently slept and had their meals there, for the stone floor was littered with straw, and empty bottles, sardine-boxes, and pieces of bread were lying about. But when I opened the door of the dining-room I could not help pausing for a moment to look at the strange sight before me. The grey light of that September morning came in through four large windows and shone dimly upon the long table. The officers of the Guard had certainly made their arrangements well. They had levied contribution upon all the silver plate that could be found, which was hardly necessary, for, as they had arrived too late to have a proper meal prepared, they had to be content with what they had brought with them. The contrast between the rich plate, some of it broken, the empty silver dishes, and the empty tins of preserved meat was strange indeed. But they had solaced themselves in the cellar. Innumerable bottles, both empty and full, were piled upon the furniture. Costly glasses of all shapes and sizes, some empty, others still half full, were standing about in every direction. The white tablecloth was soiled with large purple stains. The floor was littered with bits of smashed glass. By the table, the chairs that had been pushed back or overturned showed the number of drinkers to have been about ten. An acrid smell of tobacco and wine hung about this scene of an overnight orgy.

One thing I specially remember: the sight of an officer's cap, with a red band, hanging from one of the branches of the large chandelier in the centre of the room. And I could not help picturing to my mind the head of the man it had belonged to, some Rittmeister, with an eyeglass, fat pink cheeks and neck bulging over the collar of his tunic. What a pity he had been able to decamp! That is the kind of countenance we should so much have liked to see closer and face to face.

But I could not wait. We rushed hastily through drawing-rooms turned upside down, and bedrooms where the beds still bore traces of summary use by heavy bodies. But we found no forgotten drunkard in them.

My two corporals were already waiting for us when we returned to the courtyard. They had not found any one in their search. Quickly we mounted, and passed rapidly out by the gilded gates. The old servant and the gardener were still on the same spot, standing silent and depressed. They said not a word to us, nor did they make any sign; they seemed to be completely unhinged and incapable of understanding what had happened.

I had hardly returned to the squadron when I saw a sight I can never forget. At a turn in the road three horsemen came towards us covered with blood. I recognised F., the officer of Chasseurs d'Afrique, who had been sent out to reconnoitre the evening before. He had lost his cap, and had his head bound up with a blood-stained handkerchief. His left arm was likewise slung in an improvised bandage tied round his neck. He was followed by two men who were also covered with wounds. Their eyes shone bright and resolute in their feverish faces. One of them, having no scabbard, was still holding his sword, which was twisted and stained with blood. We pulled up instinctively and saluted.

"I haven't been able to reach the Marne," said F., with disappointment in his voice. "But, being fired upon by their outposts in the dark, we charged and got through, and then charged through two villages under a hail of bullets; and again we had to charge their outposts to get back. You see, ... I have brought back two men out of eight, and all my horses have been killed.... These horses"—pointing to his own—"are those of three Uhlans we killed so as not to have to come home on foot."

Certainly they were not riding the pretty little animals that make such excellent mounts for our Chasseurs d'Afrique, but were perched on three big mares with the heavy German equipment.

"But," F. repeated in a tone of vexation, "I wasn't able to get to the Marne.... There were too many of them for us."

We pressed his unwounded hand warmly. Poor F.! Brave fellow! Not many days afterwards he was to meet a glorious death charging once more, with three Chasseurs, to rescue one of his men who had been wounded. A more perfect type of cavalryman—I might say, of knight—was never seen. He sleeps now, riddled with lance wounds, in the plains of Champagne.

We had hardly left him when we caught sight of the reconnoitring party of my comrade O., and were overjoyed to find that he had come back unscathed with all his men. And yet he had had to face a fair number of dangers—attacks by cyclists and pursuit by cavalry. At Crézancy, where he arrived at three o'clock in the morning, he found the village occupied and strongly held. There is only one bridge over the railway there, and that is at the other end of the village. By good luck he was able to get hold of one of the inhabitants; and he forced him, by holding his revolver to his head, to guide him by all sorts of byways so as to make a circuit without attracting attention and get to the bridge. There he set forward at a gallop, and passed, in spite of being fired on by the guard. At last he reached the Marne. The only bridge he found intact for crossing the river was the bridge at Jaulgonne, a slender, fragile suspension-bridge, but one that we should be very glad to find if there was still time to use it. He then hurried back through the woods, but not without having to run the gauntlet of rifle fire several times more. He brought back information which was to guide our advance.

It was seen at once that there was not a minute to lose. The Captain detached me immediately, with my troop, to act as a flank-guard along the line of wooded crests by which the road on the right was commanded, whilst F., with his troop, crossed the Surmelin and the railway which runs alongside of it, and went to carry out the same task on the other side of the valley.

My job was difficult enough. In fact, the heights, which look down upon the course of the Surmelin to the east, consist of a series of ridges separated by narrow ravines at right angles to the river, and these we had to cross to continue our route towards the north. The enemy seemed to have withdrawn completely from this region, and the cannon fire in the distance towards the east could hardly be heard. At last, at about seven o'clock in the morning, we debouched upon the valley of the Marne.

Whilst I sent some troopers along the road which winds by the Surmelin to keep in touch with my Captain, I carefully inspected the right bank of the Marne with my glasses. The scene would have tempted a painter, and the labours of war do not prevent one from enjoying the charm of such delightful pictures. The sun was gradually dispersing the mist of the sullen morning, and was beginning to gild the wooded heights which look down upon the two banks of the river. Everywhere a calm was reigning, which seemed to promise a day of exquisite beauty. We might have fancied that we were bent on some peaceful rural work favoured by a radiant autumn morning. The Marne in this region winds in graceful curves. It flows limpid and clear through a narrow valley carpeted with green meadows and bordered, right and left, by gentle hills dotted with woods. At our feet, peeping from the poplars and beeches on the bank, we saw the white houses of dainty villages—Chartèves, Jaulgonne, Varennes, and Barzy.

I directed my attention more particularly towards Jaulgonne, because it was in that direction that the attempt to cross the river would be made. The heights immediately above Jaulgonne rise steeply on the north bank, and almost stand in the river. On the other hand, to the south, on our side, the left bank of the Marne is bordered by extensive meadows crossed by the railway and the high-road to Épernay. The position therefore would have been very strong for the Germans, if they had crossed to the other side of the river, for we should have been obliged, before we could reach the bridge, to traverse a vast open expanse which they could have kept under the fire of their artillery. My Chasseurs, prompt to grasp the reason of things, scrutinised the opposite bank no less intently than I. No movement could be seen; nothing suggested the presence of troops among the russet thickets which covered the sides of the silent hill. Could they have already retired farther off? Could they have abandoned this formidable position without any attempt to defend it?

At that moment one of my Chasseurs appeared, coming by the steep path which led from the road to the wooded ridge on which we were. His horse was panting, for the declivity was stiff, and he had had to hasten. He brought me orders.

" Mon Lieutenant, the Captain has sent me to tell you to join him as quickly as possible at the other end of the bridge. The first troop has already crossed, but some of the enemy's horse have been seen on the other side of the village."

As he said these words we heard some firing in the distance, which sounded very distinct and sharp in the radiant peace of that beautiful September morning. "Come, so much the better," thought I. "We have engaged them. We shall have a good time." My men had already begun to joke and to be more alert and abrupt in their movements. It was a kind of joyous reaction which always affects troopers when they begin to hear the guns and look forward to a good hard ride in which they, like the rest of us, are always certain of getting the best of it.

In single file we went quickly down towards the plain by the stony, slippery path. We soon reached the high-road, and then turned to the left and came upon the long causeway bordered by poplars which led to the bridge. Quite close to the bank I saw a small group of dismounted cavalrymen, and soon recognised our Colonel with his Brigade Staff. He was giving his orders to the Lieutenant-Colonel commanding the Chasseurs d'Afrique . I went up to him to report, and learnt that the first squadron had already crossed the river and occupied the village on the other side. Some parties of German cavalry had been seen on the neighbouring heights.

I got ready to rejoin my comrades at once. But patience was required if the Marne was to be crossed. The bridge appeared to be a delicate sort of toy hovering over the water. How could they dream of sending thousands of men, horses, and guns over a thing so slender that it looked as though it were supported by the fragile meshes of a spider's web? Captain D. gave me the Colonel's precise orders: not to pass more than four troopers at a time, and these at walking pace.

Taking the initiative in the movement, I started with my first four Chasseurs. The bridge rang strangely under our horses' hoofs, and seemed to me to oscillate in an alarming manner. Fortunately the enemy was not on the other side; if he had been, our passage would have cost us dear.

As I was making these reflections a violent fusillade burst out from the edge of the woods overlooking Jaulgonne to the east. It must have been directed upon the village, for no bullets whistled around us, so it was probably our first squadron engaging the German cavalry. When I got to the other end of the bridge my impatience increased. It was torture to think of the time it would take to collect my thirty men and hurry forward to help the others; and I noticed the same impatience in my men's looks. Those who were on the bridge, walking slowly and gently across, seemed to implore me to let them trot; but I pretended not to understand, and the horses' feet continued to trample heavily over the echoing bridge. At last all my men were over.

We fell in and reached Jaulgonne at a trot. On passing through it we found several of the inhabitants on their doorsteps:

" Monsieur l'Officier, ... Monsieur l'Officier, will they come back again?"

"Never!" I shouted, with conviction.

I stopped an orderly, who told me that the German cavalry were firing on the exit from the town. How many of them he could not say, as they were hidden in the woods. He told me, too, that the first squadron was holding all the entrances to the north and east of the village except the one on the river bank on the road to Marcilly, where my comrade F. had posted his troop. I decided then to put myself at the disposal of the party defending the chief exit from the village, the one that opened into the road to Fismes. It was the most important one, for it was in that direction that the Germans were retiring.

The village had been prevented from spreading further to the north by the heights, which formed an abrupt barrier. It is built astride the road to Fismes, which thus becomes its principal, if not its only, street. I had then to go right through Jaulgonne before I could get out of it in the direction of the firing. I soon did this, and found the horses of the first squadron massed in the short alleys leading out of the main street. I ordered my troop to dismount in a yard much too small and very inconvenient. But the first thing to do was to clear the causeway and shelter our horses from bullets, which might enfilade the street if the fighting bore away towards the left. Then, whilst a non-commissioned officer collected the squads for the action on foot, I ran as far as the furthest houses of the village to reconnoitre the ground and get orders.

I spied Major P. in a sheltered nook, still mounted, and he told me of his anxiety about the situation. The enemy riflemen were invisible, and were riddling the outskirts of the village, while we were unable to reply; and some guns had been seen which were being got into position. He advised me to go and see the captain of the first squadron, who had been ordered to defend that entrance of the village, and to place myself at his disposal in case of need.

Whilst we were talking, my troop, led by its non-commissioned officer, came to the place where we were, edging along by the walls. The men, calm and smiling, with their carbines ready, waited in silence for the signal to advance. I signed to them to wait a little longer, and then going round the wall I found myself suddenly in the thick of the fray. I must say the reception I got startled me. The bullets came rattling in hundreds, chipping the walls and cutting branches from the trees. On our side there was absolute silence. Our men, on their knees or lying flat behind any cover they could find, did not reply, as they could see nothing, and waited stoically under the shower of bullets until their adversaries chose to advance.

I looked for Captain de L., who commanded the first squadron. There he was, standing with his face to the enemy, and his hands in his pockets, quietly giving his orders to a non-commissioned officer. On my asking him if he wanted me, he explained the situation: the enemy, numbers unknown, was occupying the woods overlooking Jaulgonne to the east. It was impossible for us to debouch just yet. The essential thing was to hold the village, and consequently the bridge, until our infantry could come up. He told me that the first troop of my squadron, led by Lieutenant d'A., had just advanced, in extended order, into the vineyards, orchards, and fields stretching between the road and the river. He was going to reconnoitre the woods and see what kind of force was holding it.

"You see, dear fellow, for the present I don't want the

help of your carbines; I have my whole squadron here, and they can't get a shot. So long as the enemy sticks to the wood all we can do is to wait and keep our powder dry."

I put my troop under shelter in a small yard, and directed my non-commissioned officer to keep in touch with me, in case I might want him. Then I went back to the outskirts of the village to examine the ground. I then joined my friend S. behind a large heap of faggots: he commanded the nearest troop of the first squadron, and we could not help laughing at the curious situation—being formed up for battle, fronting the enemy, under a hail of bullets, and not able to see anything.

During the campaign S. had become a philosopher, and he deserved some credit for it; for the great moral and physical sufferings we had endured must have been even still more insupportable to him than to any of us. In the regiment, S. was considered preeminently the Society officer. He went to all the receptions, all the afternoon teas, all the bridge parties, all the dinners. He was an adept at tennis and golf and a first-rate shot. His elegance was proverbial, and the beautiful cut of his tunics, breeches, jackets, and coats was universally admired. The way his harness was kept and the shape of his high boots were a marvel. To say all this is to give some idea of the change he suddenly experienced in his habits and his tastes during those demoralising days of retreat and merciless hours of pursuit. But, in spite of all, he had kept his good humour and never lost his gay spirits. He still accompanied his talk with elaborate gestures, and seemed to be just as much at ease behind his heap of wood, bombarded with bullets, as in the best appointed drawing-room. His clothes were stained and patched, his beard had begun to grow, and yet under this rough exterior the polished man of the world could always be divined.

He explained the beginnings of the affair with perfect

clearness and self-possession; how the scouts sent up to the ridge by d'A. and driven off by the Germans had fallen back upon Jaulgonne; how the first squadron had come to barricade and defend the village, and in what anxiety they were waiting to know what had become of d'A.'s troop, which had started out to reconnoitre the wood.

We hoisted ourselves to the top of the faggot-stack and peeped over carefully. The glaring white road wound up the flank of the slope between fields dotted with apple trees. At a distance of 800 yards in front of us stretched the dark border of the wood, from which the fusillade was coming. To our right, at the edge of the water, on the road leading to Marcilly, F. must have been able to see the enemy, for we could distinctly hear the crackle of his carbines.

Our attention was drawn to a man of F.'s troop running along under the wall, bending almost double to escape the attention of the sniper, and endeavouring to screen himself behind the high grass. As soon as he came near enough we called out:

"What is it?"

"The Lieutenant has sent me to say that the enemy has just placed some guns in position up there, in the opening of the wood."

Saying which, he pointed vaguely in a direction where we could see nothing. However, we knew that F. would not have warned us if he had not been quite certain of the fact, so for some unpleasant minutes we wondered what the enemy's objective was. We longed to know, at once, where the projectiles were going to burst. Would it be on F.'s troop, or on the bridge, or on the infantry, which, perhaps, were beginning to debouch, or, perhaps, on that portion of the brigade that had remained dismounted on the left bank, drawn up for action? The uncertainty was worse than the danger itself. But we were not long in doubt. Two shrieks of flying shells! Two explosions about 300 yards in front of us! Two puffs of white smoke rising above the green fields! This showed they had an objective we had not considered, namely, d'A.'s troop, for the shrapnel had burst in the direction he had just taken with his men.

Our anxiety did not last long. We soon made out our Chasseurs, coming back quietly, not running, and in good order. They took to the ditch, a fairly deep one, which ran along on the left side of the road, and covered them up to the middle. The German shells were badly aimed, and exploded either in front of them or higher up on the hillside. But our anxiety became more intense every minute. Had a shell fallen on the road or in the ditch, we should have seen those brave fellows knocked over, mown down, cut to pieces, by the hail of bullets. When we are fighting ourselves we hardly have time to think about our neighbours in this way. We have our own cares, and our first thought is the safety of the men who form our little family, the troop. But when one is safe, or fairly so, it is torture to watch comrades advancing under the enemy's fire without any protection. At that moment the Germans were concentrating their fire upon that small line of men we were looking at, 200 yards away from us. The shells succeeded one another uninterruptedly, but without any greater precision. We watched our friends coming nearer until they had almost reached our barricade, and noticed that two of the Chasseurs were being supported by their comrades. In our anxiety, we got up out of shelter, but d'A. shouted: "It's nothing; only scratches...."

At last they got in, and whilst our good and indefatigable Assistant-Surgeon P. took charge of the wounded men we pressed round the officer and questioned him as to what he had seen. "Are there many of them?" "Was there any infantry?" we asked. But his daring reconnaissance had not been very fruitful. He had had to stop when the artillery had opened fire on him, and had not been able to see how many adversaries we had to deal with.

Acting on the advice of Major P., our Captain, who had just rejoined us with the third troop, gave orders to mount. We were only in the way here, where there were too many defenders already, so recrossed the bridge to put ourselves at the Colonel's disposal. I led with my troop, and we passed through Jaulgonne by the main street. The inhabitants thought we were beating a retreat and became uneasy. Some women uttered cries, begging us not to leave them at the mercy of the enemy. We had to calm them by saying that they need not fear, that we were still holding the Germans, that our infantry would soon arrive, and that in an hour the foe would have decamped.

To tell the truth, we were not quite so sure of it ourselves. The enemy was in some force, and he had guns. Our infantry had at least 15 kilometres to march before their advance guard even could debouch on the bridge at Jaulgonne. If they had not started before dawn they would not arrive before eleven o'clock, and it was then barely nine. The German artillery was already beginning to fire upon the village.

Suddenly, as we reached the market-place, we saw a group of three dismounted Chasseurs emerging from an alley that ran down steeply to the Marne. They belonged to F.'s troop. Two of them were supporting the third, whom we at once recognised. It was Laurent, a fine fellow, and a favourite with the whole squadron. It went to our hearts to see him. His left eye was nothing but a red patch, from which blood was flowing freely, drenching his clothing. He was moaning softly and, blinded by the blood, allowed himself to be led like a child. The corporal with him explained: "A bullet went in just over his eye. I don't know if the eye itself was hit."

The Captain sprang off his horse. "Cheer up, Laurent, it shall be attended to at once. Perhaps it will be nothing, my man. Come with me, we will take you to the Red Cross ambulance close by."

Then between his groans the wounded man said a thing I shall not easily forget: " Mon Capitaine, ... haven't they taken away their guns yet?"

He still took an interest in the battle. I heard afterwards that F. had sighted the German guns, and that the fire of his troop had been directed upon them. Laurent would have liked to hear that they had been driven away. He was carried off to the ambulance. I went on towards the bridge; the cannon and rifle fire still raged fiercely, but none of the shots reached the bank where we were. We had to repeat the trying process of crossing the swaying bridge by fours at walking pace. I led off with four troopers. It was not so tedious this time, as my eyes were distracted by the view of the green meadows on the opposite side.

The Colonel had disposed the brigade in such a way that he could concentrate his fire upon the bridge and the opposite bank in case we could not maintain our position there. A squadron on our left, concealed in a sand quarry, was directing its fire upon the heights where the German artillery was posted. Both up and down stream the Chasseurs d'Afrique lined the river banks, making use of every scrap of cover. Peeping out over trunks of fallen trees, banks, and ditches inquisitive heads could be seen wearing the khaki taconnet . But my troubles were not yet over. Just as I was going to step ashore from the bridge, Captain D. brought me the Colonel's orders to recross the river with my whole squadron and occupy a clump of houses to the left of the bridge. It was evidently a wise precaution. Although no firing had come from this direction, it was quite possible that some of the enemy might have slipped through the woods that come half-way down the slopes. But I did not expect such a bad time as I was going to have.

At the very moment when I was turning back, and was beginning the hateful passage for the third time, the enemy gunners, changing their objective, aimed at the bridge, and the shrapnel bullets began their disturbing music once more. Could any situation be more execrable than ours—to be upon a bridge as thin as a thread, hanging as by a miracle over a deep river, to see this bridge enfiladed by heavy musketry fire and to be obliged to walk our horses over the 200 yards which separated one bank from the other? If we had been on foot, so that we could have run and expended our strength in getting under cover—since we could not use it to defend ourselves—we should not have complained. But to be mounted on good horses, which in a few galloping strides could have carried us behind the rampart of houses, and to be obliged to hold them back instead of spurring them on, was very unpleasant, and made us feel foolish.

I looked at the four brave Chasseurs in front of me. They instinctively put up their shoulders as high as they could as if to hide their heads between them. But not one of them increased his pace. Not one of them looked round at me to beg me to give orders for a quicker advance. And what a concert was going on all the time! Whilst the horses' hoofs were beating out low and muffled notes, the bullets flew above us and around us, with shrill cracklings and whistlings which were anything but harmonious. Happily the firing was distant and disgracefully bad, for at the pace we were travelling we must have offered a very convenient mark. Another 20 yards! Ten more! At last we were safely under cover!

I communicated the Colonel's orders to the Captain, who came to join us, and directed us to occupy the little garden of a fair-sized house situated just on the edge of the Marne and the most advanced of the small group of buildings on the left-hand side of the bridge. After lodging the horses in an alley between the house and an adjoining shanty I went to reconnoitre my ground. The house was a rustic restaurant, which in the summer no doubt afforded the inhabitants an object for a walk. On passing along the terrace leading to the river I found the disorder usual in places that have been occupied by the Germans; tables overturned, bottles broken, the musty smell of empty casks, and broken crockery.

The little garden did not offer much protection for my men. However, crouching behind a kind of breastwork of earth, which shut it off from the woods, they were able, at least, to hide themselves from view. I at once posted my sharpshooters, sent out a patrol on foot as far as the entrance to the wood, and then turned my attention to what was happening near the bridge.

Whilst I was busy carrying out the Captain's orders I had not noticed that the situation had undergone a decided change, and that our chances of being able to complete our task thoroughly had increased considerably. The German guns were no longer aiming at the village. Their fire had become more rapid, and their shrapnel flew hissing over the brigade. We could see them bursting much further off, on the other side of the water, in the direction of the woods crowning the heights whence, in the morning, I had admired the smiling landscape. I inferred then that the advance guard of our corps was debouching. In half an hour it would be there, and the German cavalry, we felt sure, would not hold out much longer.

But our fine infantry had done more than this. They had, no doubt, found good roads, or perhaps the German gunners, hypnotised by the village, had not spied them. For I had now the pleasure of witnessing one of the most exhilarating spectacles I had seen since the opening of the campaign.

From where I stood on the bank I could see the thin line of the bridge above. I did not think that any one would risk crossing it now that it was known to be a mark for the enemy's fire, but suddenly I saw five men appear and begin to cross it. I could distinguish them perfectly; they were infantry soldiers, an officer and four men. The officer walked first, calmly, with a stick under his right arm, and in his left hand a map which formed a white patch on his blue coat, and behind him the men, in single file, bending slightly under their knapsacks, their caps pushed back and holding their rifles, marched firmly and steadily. They might have been on parade. Their legs could be distinguished for a moment against the blue sky. Their step was so regular that I could not help counting: one, two; one, two, as their feet struck the bridge. But just at the moment when the little group had got half-way across, a hiss, followed by a deafening explosion, made our hearts beat, and we heard the curious noise made by innumerable bullets and pieces of shell striking the water. The Germans had seen our infantry beginning to cross the river, and they were now pouring their fire upon the bridge. I looked again at the men, and saw they were there, all five of them, still marching with the same cool, resolute step: one, two; one, two. Ah! the brave fellows! How I wanted to cheer them, to shout "Bravo!" But they were too far off, and the noise of the fusillade would have prevented them from hearing me.

No sooner had they reached the bank than another little group stepped on to the narrow bridge, and then, after them, another; and each was saluted by one or two shells, with the same heavy rain of bullets falling into the water. But Providence protected our soldiers. The outline of the bridge was very slight, and the gunners of the German cavalry divisions were sorry marksmen. Their projectiles always burst either too far or too near, too high or too low. And as soon as a hundred men had got across, and the first sharpshooters had clambered up the heights that rise sheer from the river and begun to debouch upon the plateau, there was a sudden silence. The enemy's cavalry had given way, and our corps d'armée was free to pass the Marne by the bridge of Jaulgonne.

The entire battalion of the advance guard then began to pour over the bridge on their way to the plateau. Our brigade was quickly got together, and our Chasseurs hastened to water their horses. Out came the nosebags from the saddlebags. A few minutes later no one would have suspected that fighting had taken place at this spot. The men hurriedly got their snack, for we knew the halt would not last long, and that the pursuit had to be pushed till daylight failed. Our troop was in good heart and thankful that the squadron's losses had been so small. F. had just seen Laurent, the one wounded Chasseur of his troop, and said the doctors hoped to save his eye; so we had no reason to grumble.

Saddlebags were now being buckled and horses rebridled. I was to go forward to replace the troop that had led the advance guard. The Colonel sent for me and ordered me to proceed at once along the road to Fismes, search the outskirts of the village carefully, and take up a position on the heights overlooking the valley.

My troop got away quickly, and I rejoiced again at the sight of my fellows, radiant at the thought of having a dash at the enemy. We had to hasten and get ahead of the foremost parties of infantry, which also halted now for a meal. I detached my advance scouts. Their eager little horses set off at a gallop along the white road, and I was delighted to see the ease and decision with which my Chasseurs flashed out their swords. They seemed to say, "Come along, come along ...; we are ready." As for me, I rode on in quiet confidence, knowing that I had in front of me eyes keen enough to prevent any surprise.

One squad climbed nimbly up the ridge to the left. The horses scrambled up the steep ground, dislodging stones and clods of earth. They struggled with straining hocks hard to get up, and seemed to challenge each other for a race to the top. Their riders, in extended order, showed as patches of red and blue against the grey stubble. Up they went, further and further, and then disappeared over the crest. Only one was still visible, but this one was my guarantee that I had good eyes, keen and alert, on my left. Should any danger threaten from that quarter I knew well that he would pass on to me the signal received from his corporal, and I should only have to gallop to the top to judge of the situation myself. I could see the man against the blue sky, the whole outline of his body and that of his horse; the equipment and harness, the curved sword, the graceful neck, the sinewy legs, the heavy pack. I recognised the rider and knew the name of his horse. They were both of the right sort. Yes, I felt quite easy about my left.

On the right the ground dropped sheer to a narrow valley, at the bottom of which flowed a stream of clear water. Among the green trees were glittering patches here and there, on which the sun threw metallic reflections. And on the other side rose heights covered by the forest of Riz. On the edge of this forest I could see the stately ruins of a splendid country mansion. I questioned a boy who was standing on the side of the road, looking at us half timidly, half gladly.

"Tell me, child, who burnt that château over there?"

" M'sieur, they did; and they took everything away—all the beautiful things. They even carried everything off on big carts, and then they set fire to the house. But everything isn't burnt, and a lot of them came back again this morning with some horses, and they went on looking for things."

I sent off another squad towards the château, telling them first to follow the edge of the wood and to be careful how they approached it. The men got into the wood by the spaces in the bank along the road and scattered in the thickets that dotted the side of the spur we were turning. I was thus protected on my right.

I went up at a trot to the place where the road reached the plateau, and just as I was on the point of reaching it we were met by a crowd of village folk—men, women, and children—coming along, looking radiant. I saw some of them questioning my advance scouts and pointing in the direction of the north-east. It was the whole population of Le Charmel that had come out to meet us.

Le Charmel is a small village that stands at the meeting of two roads, one leading towards Fismes, the other towards Fère-en-Tardenois. It has the appearance of hanging on to the hillside, for whilst the road to Fère-en-Tardenois continues to follow the plateau, that to Fismes dips abruptly at this place and disappears in the valley. The houses of Le Charmel are perched between these two roads. Thus the people of the village had a good view of the enemy's retreat, and everybody wanted to have his say about it. I turned to a tall man, lean and tanned, with a grizzled moustache, who had something still of a military air, and seemed to be calmer than the others around him. From him I was able to get some fairly clear information.

" Mon Lieutenant, it was like this.... They went off this morning early, with a great number of cannons and horses. The artillery went straight on towards Fismes by the road. The cavalry cut across the fields, and disappeared over the ridge you see over there on the other side of the valley. Then towards eight o'clock some of them came back. How many? Well, two or three regiments perhaps, and some guns; and they went down again towards Jaulgonne. I believe they wanted to destroy the bridge. But just as they got to the turn of the hill, pan! pan!—they were fired at. Then, of course, we got back to our houses and shut them up, as the guns began to fire. But when we heard no more reports we came out again, and saw them making off across the fields like the others and in the same direction. But it is quite possible that some of them stayed in the woods, or in the farms, on the other side of the forest of Riz...."

He was interrupted by my non-commissioned officer:

" Mon Lieutenant, the scouts ... they are signalling to you...."

I galloped up to them, when they pointed out to me, at about 1,500 yards distance, on the opposite ridge, a small group of cavalrymen near a stack, and, on the side of the slope, a patrol of German dragoons, pacing slowly with lances lowered and stopping every now and then facing in our direction.

I took my glasses and looked carefully at the stack. And then I saw a sight which sent a shiver of joy through me. The horsemen had dismounted and put their horses behind the stack. Three of the men then separated themselves from the rest and formed a little group. I could not distinguish their uniforms, but saw very clearly that they were looking through their glasses at us. Now and again they put their heads together, and consulted the map, as it seemed. A man then came out from behind the stack on foot, and could be distinctly seen, against the sky, sticking into the ground by his side a square pennon which flapped gently in the breeze. As far as I could see it was half black and half white. There could be no doubt that we were confronting a Staff. So the division was not far off; it had halted, and perhaps intended this time to fight at close quarters. I told my men what I thought, and they were overjoyed at the idea that, after all, there was a hope of realising our dream. There was not one of them who doubted that the Division of the Guards had been kind enough to stop its flight, and that our brave light brigade would attack it without any hesitation and cut it to pieces. I dismounted quickly, and lost not a moment in drawing up my report. I wrote down what I had seen and what I had learnt from the inhabitants and then called one of my Chasseurs:

"To the Colonel, full gallop!"

At the touch of the spur the little chestnut turned sharp round and flew down the dusty road like a whirlwind. Meanwhile I carefully posted my men, threw out scouts over the plateau and up to the forest of Fère, and formed patrols under my non-commissioned officers. I then took up my observation post under a large tree which, to judge by its venerable look, must have seen many generations pass and many other wars. The village folk collected around me in such numbers that I was obliged to have them thrust back by my men to Le Charmel. To console them I said: "You must go away. The enemy will take you for armed troops and fire guns at you."

I kept my eye upon my "Staff," and wished my glasses could help me to distinguish more clearly what men I had to deal with. I longed to see what they were like—to examine the faces of these haughty Reiters who for the last four days had been fleeing before us and always refusing a real encounter. I fancied that among them might be found that Rittmeister with the bulging neck and pink cheeks, who, after the orgy of that night at the Château de Condé, had left behind him the cap that I had found hanging from the chandelier in the dining-room. How I longed to see the brigade debouch, and to receive instructions from the Colonel!

I had not long to wait. My messenger soon came back, trotting up the road from Jaulgonne. But the instructions were not what I had expected. I was to stay where I was until further orders, to continue to observe the enemy, and keep a look-out in his direction.

I learnt some details from the man. The greater part of the infantry had already crossed the bridge, and there was also some artillery on this side of the river. As he said this a clatter of wheels and chains caused me to turn my head, and I saw behind us, in the stubble-fields of the plateau, two batteries of 75's taking up positions. Ah! ah! we were going to send them our greetings then, a salute to the pompous General over there, and to his aide-de-camp, the stiff and obsequious Rittmeister, whom I imagined to be at his side. I looked on gaily with my Chasseurs at the laying of the guns. How we all loved that good little gun, which had so often come up to lend us the support of its terrible projectiles at critical moments! And those good fellows the gunners loved it too; the men we saw jumping nimbly down from their limber, quickly unhitching their piece, and pointing it with tender care towards the enemy.

Standing on a bank, with his glasses to his eyes, the officer in command gave his orders which were passed from man to man by the markers. And then suddenly we heard four loud, sharp reports behind us. The whistling of the shells, which almost grazed our heads, was impressive, and, though we knew there was no danger, we instinctively ducked. But we recovered ourselves at once to see what effect they had produced.

What a pity! They had fallen a bit short. We distinctly saw four small white puffs on the side of the hill just below the group of German officers. Ah! They didn't wait for another! I saw them make off in hot haste whilst the troopers, stationed behind the stack, galloped off the horses. The man with the flag was the last to go, closing the procession with rather more dignity. But in ten seconds the whole lot had decamped, and the only men we could see were the dragoons of the patrol, who rode back to the ridge at full speed.

But just as they reached it the second battery opened fire, and this time the sighting was just right. The four white puffs appeared exactly over the spot where the Staff had stood a minute before—two to the right and two to the left of the stack. And all we now saw of the patrol was two riderless horses galloping madly towards the woods. Then the two batteries pounded away with a will.

When I had received orders to resume the forward movement and my good Chasseurs had taken up the pursuit again, the gunners had lengthened their range with mathematical precision, and the shells burst on the farther side of the ridge. I took a grim pleasure in imagining what must have been happening there, where, no doubt, the division was drawn up, and whilst I continued to direct my vigilant and expert scouts I amused myself by picturing the brilliant troopers of the Prussian Guard in headlong flight.

Chapter 5
Low Mass and Benediction
September, 1914

One morning in the middle of September, 1914, as we raised our heads at about six o'clock from the straw on which we had slept, I and my friend F. had a very disagreeable surprise: we heard in the darkness the gentle, monotonous noise of water falling drop by drop from the penthouse roof on to the road.

Arriving at Pévy the evening before, just before midnight, we had found refuge in a house belonging to a peasant. The hostess, a good old soul of eighty, had placed at our disposal a small bare room paved with tiles, in which our orderlies had prepared a sumptuous bed of trusses of straw. The night had been delightful, and we should have awaked in good spirits had it not been for the distressing fact noticed by my friend.

"It is raining," said F.

I could not but agree with him. Those who have been soldiers, and especially cavalrymen, know to the full how dispiriting is the sound of those few words: "It is raining."

"It is raining" means your clothes will be saturated; your cloak will be drenched, and weigh at least forty pounds; the water will drip from your shako along your neck and down your back; above all, your high boots will be transformed into two little pools in which your feet paddle woefully. It means broken roads, mud splashing you up to the eyes, horses slipping, reins stiffened, your saddle transformed into a hip-bath. It means that the little clean linen you have brought with you—that precious treasure—in your saddlebags, will be changed into a wet bundle on which large and indelible yellow stains have been made by the soaked leather.

But it was no use to think of all this. The orders ran: "Horses to be saddled, and squadron ready to mount, at 6.30." And they had to be carried out.

It was still dark. I went out into the yard, after pulling down my campaigning cap over my ears. Well, after all, the evil was less than I had feared. It was not raining, but drizzling. The air was mild, and there was not a breath of wind. When once our cloaks were on it would take some hours for the wet to reach our shirts. At the farther end of the yard some men were moving about round a small fire. Their shadows passed to and fro in front of the ruddy light. They were making coffee— jus, as they call it—that indispensable ration in which they soak bread and make a feast without which they think a man cannot be a good soldier.

I ran to my troop through muddy alleys, skipping from side to side to avoid the puddles. Daylight appeared, pale and dismal. A faint smell rose from the sodden ground.

"Nothing new, mon Lieutenant," were the words that greeted me from the sergeant, who then made his report. I had every confidence in him; he had been some years in the service, and knew his business. Small and lean, and tightly buttoned into his tunic, in spite of all our trials he was still the typical smart light cavalry non-commissioned officer. I knew he had already gone round the stables, which he did with a candle in his hand, patting the horses' haunches and looking with a watchful eye to see whether some limb had not been hurt by a kick or entangled in its tether.

In the large yard of the abandoned and pillaged farm,

where the men had been billeted they were hurrying to fasten the last buckles and take their places in the ranks. I quickly swallowed my portion of insipid lukewarm coffee, brought me by my orderly; then I went to get my orders from the Captain, who was lodged in the market-square. No word had yet been received from the Colonel, who was quartered at the farm of Vadiville, two kilometres off. Patience! We had been used to these long waits since the army had been pulled up before the formidable line of trenches which the Germans had dug north of Reims. They were certainly most disheartening; but it could not be helped, and it was of no use to complain. I turned and went slowly up the steep footpath that led to my billet.

Pévy is a poor little village, clinging to the last slopes of a line of heights that runs parallel to the road from Reims to Paris. Its houses are huddled together, and seem to be grouped at the foot of the ridges for protection from the north wind. The few alleys which intersect the village climb steeply up the side of the hill. We were obliged to tramp about in the sticky mud of the main road waiting for our orders.

Passing the church, it occurred to me to go and look inside. Since the war had begun we had hardly had any opportunity of going into the village churches we had passed. Some of them were closed because the parish priests had left for the army, or because the village had been abandoned to the enemy. Others had served as marks for the artillery, and now stood in the middle of the villages, ruins loftier and more pitiable than the rest.

The church of Pévy seemed to be clinging to the side of the hill, and was approached by a narrow stairway of greyish stone, climbing up between moss-grown walls. I first passed through the modest little churchyard, with its humble tombs half hidden in the grass, and read some of the simple inscriptions:

"Here lies ... Here lies ... Pray for him...."

The narrow pathway leading to the porch was almost hidden in the turf, and as I walked up it my boots brushed the drops from the grass. The damp seemed to be getting into my bones, for it was still drizzling—a fine persistent drizzle. Behind me the village was in mist; the roofs and the maze of chimney tops were hardly distinguishable.

Passing through a low, dark porch, I opened the heavy door studded with iron nails, and entered the church, and at once experienced a feeling of relaxation, of comfort and repose. How touching the little sanctuary of Pévy seemed to me in its humble simplicity!

Imagine a kind of hall with bare walls, the vault supported by two rows of thick pillars. The narrow Gothic windows hardly allowed the grey light to enter. There were no horrible cheap modern stained windows, but a multitude of small white rectangular leaded panes. All this was simple and worn; but to me it seemed to breathe a noble and touching poetry. And what charmed me above all was that the pale light did not reveal walls covered with the horrible colour-wash we are accustomed to see in most of our village churches.

This church was an old one, a very old one. Its style was not very well defined, for it had no doubt been built, damaged, destroyed, rebuilt and repaired by many different generations. But those who preserved it to the present day had avoided the lamentable plastering which disfigures so many others. The walls were built with fine large stones, on which time had left its melancholy impress. There was no grotesque painting on them to mar their quiet beauty, and the dim light that filtered through at that early hour gave them a vague soft glow.

No pictures or ornaments disfigured the walls. The "Stations of the Cross" were the only adornment, and they were so simple and childish in their execution that they were no doubt the work of some rustic artist. And even this added a touching note to a harmonious whole.

But my attention was attracted by a slight noise, a kind of soft and monotonous murmur, coming from the altar. The choir was almost in darkness, but I could distinguish the six stars of the lighted candles. In front of the tabernacle was standing a large white shadowy form, almost motionless and like a phantom. At the bottom of the steps another form was kneeling, bowed down towards the floor; it did not stir as I approached. I went towards the choir on tiptoe, very cautiously. I felt that I, a profane person, was committing a sacrilege by coming to disturb those two men praying there all alone in the gloom of that sad morning. A deep feeling of emotion passed through me, and I felt so insignificant in their presence and in the mysterious atmosphere of the place that I knelt down humbly, almost timidly, in the shadow of one of the great pillars near the altar.

Then I could distinguish my fellow-worshippers better. A priest was saying mass. He was young and tall, and his gestures as he officiated were slow and dignified. He did not know that some one was present watching him closely; so it could not be supposed that he was speaking and acting to impress a congregation, and yet he had a way of kneeling, of stretching out his arms and of looking up to the humble gilded cross in front of him, that revealed all the ardour of fervent prayers. Occasionally he turned towards the back of the church to pronounce the ritual words. His face was serious and kindly, framed in a youthful beard—the face of an apostle, with the glow of faith in his eyes. And I was surprised to see underneath his priest's vestments the hems of a pair of red trousers, and feet shod in large muddy military boots.

The kneeling figure at the bottom of the steps now stood out more distinctly. The man was wearing on his shabby infantry coat the white armlet with the red cross. He must have been a priest, for I could distinguish some traces of a neglected tonsure among his brown hair.

The two repeated, in a low tone by turns, words of prayer, comfort, repentance, or supplication, harmonious Latin phrases, which sounded to me like exquisite music. And as an accompaniment in the distance, in the direction of Saint Thierry and Berry-au-Bac, the deep voice of the guns muttered ceaselessly.

For the first time in the campaign I felt a kind of poignant melancholy. For the first time I felt small and miserable, almost a useless thing, compared with those two fine priestly figures who were praying in the solitude of this country church for those who had fallen and were falling yonder under shot and shell.

How I despised and upbraided myself at such moments! What a profound disgust I felt for the follies of my garrison life, its gross pleasures and silly excesses! I was ashamed of myself when I reflected that death brushed by me every day, and that I might disappear to-day or to-morrow, after so many ill-spent and unprofitable days.

Without any effort, and almost in spite of myself, pious words came back to my lips—those words that my dear mother used to teach me on her knee years and years ago. And I felt a quiet delight in the almost forgotten words that came back to me:

"Forgive us our trespasses.... Pray for us, poor sinners...."

It seemed to me that I should presently go away a better man and a more valiant soldier. And, as though to encourage and bless me, a faint ray of sunshine came through the window.

"Ite, missa est...." The priest turned round; and this time I thought his eyes rested upon me, and that the look was a benediction and an absolution.

But suddenly I heard in the alley close by a great noise of people running and horses stamping, and a voice crying:

"Mount horses!... Mount horses!"

I was sorry to leave the little church of Pévy; I should so much have liked to wait until those two priests came out, to speak to them, and talk about other things than war, massacres and pillage. But duty called me to my men, my horses, and to battle.

Shortly afterwards, as I passed at the head of my troop in front of the large farm where the ambulance of the division was quartered, I saw my abbé coming out of a barn, with his sleeves tucked up and his képi on the side of his head. He was carrying a large pail of milk. I recognised his clear look, and had no doubt that he recognised me too, for as our eyes met he gave me a kindly smile.

My heart was lighter as I went forward, and my soul was calmer.

*****

For the last six days we had been quartered at Montigny-sur-Vesle, a pretty little village half-way up a hillside on the heights, 20 kilometres to the west of Reims. There we enjoyed a little rest for the first time in the campaign. On our front the struggle was going on between the French and German trenches, and the employment of cavalry was impossible. All the regiment had to do was to supply daily two troops required to ensure the connection between the two divisions of the army corps.

What a happiness it was to be able at last to enjoy almost perfect rest! What a delight to lie down every evening in a good bed; not to get up before seven o'clock; to find our poor horses stabled at last on good litter in the barns, and to see them filling out daily and getting sleeker!

For our mess we had the good luck to find a most charming and simple welcome at the house of good Monsieur

Cheveret. That kind old gentleman did everything in his power to supply us with all the comforts he could dispose of. And he did it all with such good grace and such a pleasant smile that we felt at ease and at home at once. Madame Cheveret, whom we at once called "Maman Cheveret," was an alert little old lady who trotted about all day long in quest of things to do for us. She put us up in the dining-room, and helped our cook to clean the vegetables and to superintend the joints and sweets. For Gosset, the bold Chasseur appointed to preside over our mess arrangements, was a professional in the culinary art, and excelled in making everything out of nothing; so, with the help of Maman Cheveret, he accomplished wonders, and the result of it all was that we began to be enervated by the delights of this new Capua. And how thoroughly we enjoyed it!

We shared our Eden with two other squadrons of our regiment, a section of an artillery park, and a divisional ambulance. We prayed Heaven to grant us a long stay in such a haven of repose.

Now one morning, after countless ablutions with hot water and a clean shave, I was going, with brilliantly shining boots, down the steep footpath which led to the little house of our good Monsieur Cheveret, when my attention was drawn to a small white notice posted on the door of the church. It ran: *This evening at six o'clock, benediction of the most Holy Sacrament.*

It occurred to me at once that this happy idea had been conceived by the Chaplain of the Ambulance, for until then the church had been kept locked, as the young parish priest had been called up by the mobilisation. I made haste to tell our Captain and my comrades the good news, and we all determined to be present at the Benediction that evening.

At half-past five our ears were delighted by music such as we had not been accustomed to hear for a very long time. In the deepening twilight some invisible hand was chiming the bells of the little church. How deliciously restful they were after the loud roar of the cannon and the rattle of the machine-guns! Who would have thought that such deep, and also such solemn, notes could come from so small a steeple? It stirred the heart and brought tears to the eyes, like some of Chopin's music. Those bells seemed to speak to us, they seemed to call us to prayer and preach courage and virtue to us.

At the end of the shady walk I was passing down—whose trees formed a rustling wall on either side—appeared the little church, with its slender steeple. It stood out in clear relief, a dark blue, almost violet silhouette against the purple background made by the setting sun. Some dark human forms were moving about and collecting around the low arched doorway. Perhaps these were the good old women of the district who had come to pray in this little church which had remained closed to them for nearly two months. I fancied I could distinguish them from where I was, dignified and erect in their old-fashioned mantles.

But as soon as I got closer to them I found I was mistaken. It was not aged and pious women who were hurrying to the church door, but a group of silent artillerymen wrapped in their large blue caped cloaks. The bells shook out their solemn notes, and seemed to be calling others to come too; and I should have been glad if their voices had been heard, for I was afraid the Chaplain's appeal would hardly be heeded and that the benches of the little church would be three-parts empty.

But on gently pushing the door open I found at once that my fears were baseless. The church was in fact too small to hold all the soldiers, who had come long before the appointed hour as soon as they heard the bells begin. And now that I had no fears about the church being empty

I wondered how I was going to find a place myself. I stood on the doorstep, undecided, on tip-toe, looking over the heads of all those standing men to see whether there was any corner unoccupied where I could enjoy the beauty of the unexpected sight in peace.

The nave was almost dark. The expense of lighting, had no doubt to be considered, for for several days past no candle or taper was to be had for money. And no doubt the kindness of a motorist of the Red Cross had been appealed to for the supply of all the candles which lit up the altar. This was indeed resplendent. The vestry had been ransacked for candlesticks, and the tabernacle was surrounded by a splendid aureole of light. All this increased the touching impression I felt on entering.

Against the brilliant background of the choir stood out the black forms of several hundreds of men standing and looking towards the altar. Absolute silence reigned over the whole congregation of soldiers. And yet no discipline was enforced; there was no superior present to impose a show of devotion. Left to themselves, they all understood what they had to do. They crowded together, waiting in silence and without any impatience for the ceremony to begin.

Suddenly a white figure came towards me through the crowded ranks of soldiers. He extended his arms in token of welcome, and I at once recognised the Chaplain in his surplice. His face was beaming with pleasure, and his eyes shone behind his spectacles. He appeared to be supremely happy.

"This way, Monsieur l'Officier, this way. I have thought of everything. You must have the seat of honour. Follow me."

I followed the holy man, who elbowed a way for me up the crowded aisle. He had reserved all the choir-stalls for the officers. Before the war they had been occupied, at high mass, by the clergy, the choir, and the principal members of the congregation. He proudly showed me into one of them, and I felt rather embarrassed at finding myself suddenly in a blaze of light between an artillery lieutenant and a surgeon-major.

The low vestry door now opened and a very unexpected procession appeared. In front of a bearded priest walked four artillerymen in uniform. One of them carried a censer, and another the incense-box. The other two walked in front of them, arms crossed and eyes front. The whole procession knelt before the altar with perfect precision, and I saw beneath the priest's vestments muddy gaiters of the same kind as those worn by the gunners.

At the same time we heard, quite close to us, strains of music which seemed to us celestial. In the dim light I had not noticed the harmonium, but now I could distinguish the artist who was enchanting us by his skill in drawing sweet sounds from a poor worn instrument. He was an artillery captain. At once all eyes were turned towards him; we were all enraptured. None of us dared to hope that we should lift our voices in the hymns.

The organist seemed unconscious of his surroundings. The candle placed near the keyboard cast a strange light upon the most expressive of heads. Against the dark background of the church the striking features of a noble face were thrown into strong relief: a forehead broad and refined, an aristocratic nose, a fair moustache turned up at the ends, and, notably, two fine blue eyes, which, without a glance at the fingers on the keys, were fixed on the vaulted roof as though seeking inspiration there.

The Chaplain, turning to the congregation, then said:

"My friends, we will all join in singing the O Salutaris ."

The harmonium gave the first notes, and I braced myself to endure the dreadful discords I expected from this crowd of soldiers—mostly reservists—who, I supposed, had come together that evening mainly out of curiosity.

Judge of my astonishment! At first only a few timid voices joined the Chaplain's. But after a minute or so a marvel happened. From all those chests came a volume of sound such as I could hardly have believed possible. Who will say then that our dear France has lost her Faith? Who can believe it? Every one of these men joined in singing the hymn, and not one of them seemed ignorant of the Latin words. It was a magnificent choir, under a lofty vault, chanting with the fervour of absolute sincerity. There was not one discordant note, not one voice out of tune, to spoil its perfect harmony.

Who can believe that men, many of them more than thirty years old, would remember all the words unless they had been brought up in the faith of their ancestors and still held it?

I could not help turning to look at them. In the light of the candles their faces appeared to be wonderfully transfigured. Not one of them expressed irony or even indifference. What a fine picture it would have made for a Rembrandt! The bodies of the men were invisible in the darkness of the nave, and their heads alone emerged from the gloom. The effect was grand enough to fascinate the most sceptical of painters; it soothed and charmed one and wiped out all the miseries that the war had left in its wake. Men like these would be equal to anything, ready for anything; and I myself should much have liked to see a Monsieur Homais hidden away in some corner of that church.

Meanwhile the sacred Office was proceeding at the altar. At any other time we might have smiled at the sight of that soldier-priest served by choristers of thirty-five in uniform; at that ceremony it was inexpressibly touching and attractive, and it was especially delightful to see how carefully and precisely each performed his function that the ceremony might not lack its accustomed pomp.

When the singing had ceased the Chaplain went up to the holy table. In a voice full of feeling he tried to express his gratitude and happiness to all those brave fellows. I should not imagine him to be a brilliant speaker at the best of times, but on that occasion the worthy man was completely unintelligible. His happiness was choking him. He tried in vain to find the words he wanted, used the wrong ones, and only confused himself by trying to get them right. But nobody had the least desire to laugh when, to conclude his address, he said with a sigh of relief:

"And now we will tell twenty beads of the rosary; ten for the success of our arms, and the other ten in memory of soldiers who have died on the field of honour.... Hail! Mary, full of grace ...."

I looked round the church once more, and every one's lips were moving silently accompanying the priest's words. Opposite us I saw the artillery captain take a rosary out of his pocket and tell the beads with dreamy eyes; and when the Chaplain came to the sentence "Holy Mary, Mother of God, ..." hundreds of voices burst forth, deep and manly voices, full of fervour which seemed to proclaim their faith in Him Who was present before them on the altar, and also to promise self-sacrifice and devotion to that other sacred thing, their Country.

Then, after the Tantum ergo had been sung with vigour, the priest held up the monstrance, and I saw all those soldiers with one accord kneel down on the stone floor and bow their heads. The silence was impressive; not a word, not a cough, and not a chair moved. I had never seen such devotion in any church. Some spiritual power was brooding over the assemblage and bowing all those heads in token of submission and hope. Good, brave soldiers of France, how we love and honour you at such moments, and what confidence your chiefs must feel when they lead such men to battle!

*****

We sat at table around the lamp, and good Maman Cheveret had just brought in the steaming soup. Right away towards the east we heard the dull roll of the cannon. Good Monsieur Cheveret had just brought up from his cellar a venerable bottle of his best Burgundy, and, at the invitation of the Captain, he sat down to drink a glass with us, smoking his cherry-wood pipe and listening with delight to our merry chat.

Gosset was in his kitchen next door preparing a delicious piece of beef à la mode and at the same time telling the admiring Maman Cheveret about his exploits of the past month.

We heard the men of the first troop cracking their jokes in the yard as they ate their rations and emptied their pannikin of wine under a brilliant moon.

Down in the valley on the banks of the murmuring Vesle, songs and laughter floated up to us from the artillery park.

And the village itself, shining under the starlit sky, seemed bathed in an atmosphere of cheerfulness, courage and confidence.

Chapter 6

A TRAGIC NIGHT IN THE TRENCHES

November 3rd, 1914

Imagine a little tiled room, some 16 feet by 9, in which for over a fortnight passing soldiers have been living, sleeping, and eating; imagine the furniture overturned, the broken crockery strewn on the floor, the doors and drawers of the cupboards pulled out, their modest contents scattered to the four corners of the house; add to this windows without glass, doors broken in, rubbish of every kind lying about, brought no one can tell whence or how; and yet note that one or two chromo-lithographs, a few photographs of friends and relatives and certain familiar objects, still cling to the walls, evoking the life that animated this home but a short time ago, and you will get some idea of the place where my Major, my comrades of the squadron and I were lodged on that memorable November evening.

It was five o'clock, and night was already falling, the cold, damp, misty night of Flanders following on a dreary autumn day. Outside the guns were roaring far away. The Battle of the Yser was going on.

Our regiment had just been brought by rail from the Reims district, where it was, to the North of France, and thence to Belgium. Our chiefs had said: "You must leave your horses, you must forget that you ever were cavalrymen, you must make up your minds cheerfully to your new calling and become infantrymen for the time being.

We are short of infantry here, and the Germans are trying to rush Dunkirk and Calais. Your country relies upon you to stop them." Our good Chasseurs left their horses at Elverdinghe, 10 kilometres from here. They came on foot, hampered by their heavy cavalry cloaks, dragging their riding boots through the atrocious mud of the ruined roads, carrying in their packs, together with their ration of bread and tinned meat, the huge load of one hundred and twenty cartridges; they arrived here in the firing line, and quite simply, as if they had never been accustomed to anything else, did wonders there and then.

Yesterday, I grieve to say, I was not at the head of my troop. I was unable to take part in the epic battle round Bixschoote, the poor Belgian village which was retaken and then abandoned by us for the twentieth time. I was not present at the heroic death of the gallant and charming Colonel d'A., of the—Chasseurs, the author of those heart-stirring pages—and among them "The Charge"—which bring tears to the eyes of every cavalryman. He died facing the enemy, leading his regiment to the attack under terrific fire, and when his men carried him away they ranged themselves round him to make a rampart of their bodies for the chief they adored. I was not able to share the danger of my young comrade, Second-Lieutenant J., who fell bravely at the head of his marksmen, in the middle of my beloved regiment, in which fresh gaps have been made by the enemy's bullets. My seniority had marked me out as officer of liaison to the General commanding our division. But this morning at dawn I came back to take my place in the firing line, and I think I shall be able to make up for lost time.

The day has been absolutely quiet, however. After the fighting of the day before, and a night of sleeplessness and incessant alarms in the trenches, three of our squadrons, mine among them, were relieved before dawn and placed in reserve. They found billets in little forsaken farms some 600 yards from the firing line. Our men rested as well as they could all day, making beds of the scanty supplies of straw they found, washing themselves in pools, and renewing their strength in order to relieve the troops which had remained in the trenches; a squadron of our regiment, a squadron of the—Chasseurs, and a section of infantry Chasseurs.

Seated on a broken box, I was doing my best to write a letter, while Major B. and my brother officers O. and F., together with Captain de G., of the third squadron, took their seats at a rickety table and began a game of bridge. Here, by the way, is a thing passing the understanding of the profane, I mean the non-bridge player. This is the extraordinary, I might almost say the immoderate, attraction which the initiated find in this game, even at the height of a campaign. What inexhaustible joys it must offer to make its adepts profit by the briefest moments of respite in a battle to settle down anywhere and anyhow and give themselves up to their mysterious practices!

I pause for a moment in my letter-writing to enjoy the sight, which has its special charm. Two or three kilometres off, towards Steenstraate, the cannon were working away furiously, while only a few paces from our shanty a section of our 75's was firing incessantly over the wood upon Bixschoote; overhead we heard the unpleasant roar of the big German shells; and in the midst of the racket I saw my bridge players dragging their table over to the broken window. Day was dying, and we had not seen a gleam of sunshine since morning. The sky was grey—a thick, dirty grey; it seemed to be very low, close upon us, and I felt that the night would come by slow degrees without any of those admirable symphonies of colour that twilight sometimes brings to battlefields, making the combatant feel that he is ending his day in apotheosis.

But those four seemed to hear nothing. In the grey light

I watched the refined profile of the Major bending over the cards just dealt by F. He no doubt has to speak first, for the three others looked at him, in motionless silence, as if they were expecting some momentous utterance. Then suddenly, accompanied by the muffled roar of the battle music, the following colloquy took place, a colloquy full of traps and ambushes, I suppose, for the four officers cast suspicious and inquisitorial glances at each other over their cards:

"One spade." "Two hearts." "Two no trumps." "I double." "Your turn, Major."

But all of a sudden paf! paf! The four players had thrown down their cards, and we all looked at each other without a word. Suddenly we had just heard above us that strange and indefinable crackle made by bullets fired at close range as they tear through the air just above one. No doubt was possible; something extraordinary was happening near the trenches, for the crackling increased mightily, and hundreds and hundreds of bullets began to whistle round us. F. sent the table rolling to the other end of the room with a kick, and we all rushed out after the Major.

There is no more depressing moment in warfare than when one finds oneself exposed to violent fire from the enemy without being able to see whence it comes, or what troops are firing, and what is its objective. Obviously the attack was not directed against us, for between the trenches and the houses where we were there was a thick wood which entirely concealed us from the sight of the enemy. But on the other hand the shots could not have been fired from the trenches the Germans had hitherto occupied opposite us, for had they been the bullets must have passed high over our heads, and we should have heard only the characteristic whistle of shots fired at long range.

For a moment, only a moment, we were full of dread. What had happened? What had become of the comrades who were in the firing-line? Grouped together in the little enclosure bordered with quick-set hedges where there were still traces of what had been the kitchen-garden of our farm, we strained our eyes to see without uttering a word. In front of us was the dark line of the wood. We scrutinised it sharply, this silent mass of trees and bushes on which autumn had already laid the most splendid colours of its palette. In spite of the dull light, what an admirable background it made to the melancholy picture of the devastated landscape! First, quite close to the ground, was a tangle of bushes and brambles, its russet foliage forming a kind of impenetrable screen, which, in bright sunshine, would have been a curtain of purple and gold. Then, pointing up into the misty sky, came the denuded trunks of the trees, surrounded by a maze of myriads of delicate branches, their ramifications stretching a violet-tinted veil across the sky. In spite of the tragic present I could not but admire the marvellous setting Nature offered for the drama in which we were destined to be the actors.

The bullets continued their infernal music, whistling in thousands over our heads. At the same time the fire of the German mortars redoubled in intensity, and their great "coal-boxes" (big shells) burst with a deafening din a few hundred yards behind us, seeking to silence our guns. These, concealed in a hollow, answered vigorously.

But what did it all mean? What was happening? We longed to shout, to call, to implore some one to answer us, to tell us what had been taking place behind the thick curtain of the wood. But the curtain remained impenetrable.

In the few seconds we spent below that deserted house in the little trampled garden-close, under the rain of bullets that was falling around us, one dread oppressed us, and lay so heavy on our hearts that it made us dumb and incapable of exchanging our thoughts, or, rather, the one thought that haunted us all. "What has become of the second squadron? What has become of our Colonel, who had stayed in command? What has become of all our dear fellows there on the other side of the wood?" Uncertainty is indeed the worst of all miseries, because it makes its victims believe and imagine every horror.

From our post we could see at the windows and doors of the little houses scattered among the fields the anxious and inquiring faces of our men. They, too, were tortured by uncertainty. They stood huddled together, looking in our direction, waiting for a sign or an order.

Suddenly our doubts were dissipated.

"To arms!" cried our Major, in a ringing voice that echoed above the crackling of the bullets and was heard by the whole squadron.

He had no need to repeat the order. In the twinkling of an eye my troop had formed behind me, in squads. My men waited in absolute silence, their eyes fixed upon me, kneeling on one knee, and leaning on their rifles. I seemed to hear all their hearts beating in unison with mine; and knew their wills ready to second mine.

The Major gave the word of command. We disposed our men in skirmishing order in the ditch of the road that passed in front of our farm, parallel with the skirts of the wood. Our squadrons thus formed a line of from 300 to 400 yards, capable of holding the enemy in check for some time, if they had succeeded in taking our trenches and were already pushing through the thicket. Kneeling on the road behind them, I looked at my men. They were lying flat on the ground on the slope of the ditch; they had loaded their rifles, and I could not distinguish the slightest trace of fear or even of emotion in any one of them.

They were all looking straight before them trying to see whether some helmeted soldier were emerging from the bushes in the gathering shadow. What splendid soldiers the war has fashioned for us! They are no longer merely the diligent and conscientious cavalrymen we took pleasure in commanding, and whose smartness we admired in peace time. The stern experience of the battlefield has hardened, strengthened and ennobled them. Their faces are manlier; their discipline, far from relaxing, has become more thorough; their courage has developed, and, in most of them, now verges on temerity.

I have had two new men in my troop for a short time: Ladoucette and Roger. They are Territorials, men of from thirty-eight to forty, who, wearying of the depôt and envying their juniors in the field, asked and obtained leave to rejoin the regiment at the Front. They fascinated me at once by their high spirits, their jovial chaff, and the cheerfulness with which they undertook the most laborious tasks. But I had not yet seen them under fire.

I looked about for them in the line of skirmishers. I tried to distinguish them among all the backs and necks lying before me. And I very soon guessed that they were at the extreme right of the troop, for I heard smothered laughter at that corner; evidently Ladoucette was cracking some of the highly-spiced jokes characteristic of him. Yes, I saw his head lifted above the grass on the slope, his bristling moustache, his brilliant eyes, and sarcastic mouth. I could not hear what he was saying, for the firing was still furious, but I saw from the smiling faces of his neighbours that he had, as usual, found the right word for the occasion, the word that provokes laughter under bullet fire and makes men forget danger. Not far from him his inseparable chum, Roger, guffawed appreciatively, and seemed to be enjoying himself thoroughly. I rejoiced to think that I had got two first-rate recruits, worthy to fight side by side with the fine fellows of my brave troop.

Suddenly a dark figure emerged from the wood, then

two more, then another three, then more. Was it the enemy? Without waiting for the word of command some of the men pointed their rifles at the mysterious shadows running in single file towards us.

"Don't fire! Don't fire!"

We had, fortunately, recognised the uniform of our infantry Chasseurs. But this increased rather than allayed our anxiety. We naturally imagined the direst catastrophes and feared the most terrible consequences when we saw those in whom we had trusted, those who occupied the trenches nearest to Bixschoote, beating a retreat. The first of the fugitives came up to us. They seemed completely demoralised. Haggard, ragged, and black with dust, they crossed the road at a run. We tried in vain to stop them. As they passed us they shouted something unintelligible, of which we could catch nothing but the words:

"They're coming, ... they're coming."

Together with O., I succeeded in stopping two men, who were going along less rapidly, supporting a wounded comrade who was groaning and dragging himself on one leg.

"Our flank was turned; there are thousands of them. They came through the village and enfiladed us. We had a great many killed ... our officer wounded. We must get back further to the rear."

As they went off haltingly with their comrade, whose groans were pitiable to hear, the tall figure of a lieutenant of foot Chasseurs rose suddenly before us. He looked like a ghost, and for a moment we thought he was about to fall, an exhausted mass, at our feet. His face was covered with blood. The red mask in which the white of the eyes formed two brilliant spots was horrible to see. His torn tunic and all his clothing were saturated with blood. He was gesticulating wildly with the revolver he clutched in his hands, and seemed absolutely distraught.

As he passed the Major seized him by the arm:

"Halt! halt! Look here, you must rally your men. We can put up a good defence here."

The officer wrenched himself free, and went off with hasty strides, calling to us without turning his head:

"I know what I must do.... We can't hold a line here.... I am going to form up by the artillery."

Two more men came by, depressed and silent, bent down by the weight of their knapsacks. They crossed the ditches by the roadside with difficulty, and were presently lost to sight in the fields amidst the gathering shadows.

There was no laughter now in our ranks. The same thought was in every mind, the same despair chilled every heart. The Germans must have taken our trenches, and our brave comrades had all chosen to die rather than to retreat. And the enemy must be there before us, in that wood; they must be stealing up to us noiselessly. I fancied I could see them, gliding from tree to tree, holding their rifles high, trying to deaden the sound of their footsteps among the dead leaves. Presently they would reach the dark line that stretched before us, mute and mysterious; they would mass their dense reserves in the rear, and suddenly thousands of lightning flashes would illuminate the fringe of the thicket. I looked at my men again. There was no sign of wavering; not a word was spoken; their faces looked a little pale in the waning light. Above us thousands of shells and bullets filled the air with their strange and terrible music.

A man came out of the wood and walked quietly towards us. It was not light enough to distinguish his uniform, but his calm and placid bearing was in marked contrast to that of the infantry Chasseurs. He must have recognised the little group formed by the Major, my comrades, and myself in the middle of the road, for he made straight for us.

When he got to within twenty paces of us we recognised

to our joy Sergeant Madelin, a non-commissioned officer of our second squadron, the squadron that had stayed in the trenches with the Colonel and the machine-gun section. I cannot describe the relief we felt at the sight of him. Though we could not tell what he was going to say, his attitude dispelled our fears at once. He gazed at us with wide astonished eyes from under the peak of his shako, and came on quietly, as if he were taking a walk, his hands in his pockets, murmuring in a tone of stupefaction:

"What on earth is the matter?"

"Well, really, this is a little too much!" exclaimed the Major; "that's just what we want you to tell us !"

"But I have nothing to tell you, Major. The trench of the infantry Chasseurs was taken. We are all right. But the Colonel has sent me to say that there are signs of a German counter-attack on the left, and he wants you to reinforce him on that side with your three squadrons."

He spoke so calmly and with such an air of astonishment that we all felt inclined to laugh. Madelin had already given proof of his courage, he had even been mentioned in orders for his valour, but we had never seen him so placidly good-humoured under fire as on this occasion. All our fears were at once put to flight, and we thought only of one thing; to fly to the help of our comrades and win our share of glory.

"Forward!"

The officers had advanced in front of the line of skirmishers. All the men sprang up in an instant, and the three squadrons dashed forward full speed.

But at the exact moment when our men, springing out of the ditches, began their advance towards the wood, the enemy's artillery, shortening its range, began to pour a perfect hail of shrapnel on our line. It was now almost pitch dark, and there was something infernal in the scene. The shells were bursting at a considerable height above us, some in front, some behind. They made a horrible kind of music. There must have been at least two batteries at work upon us, for we could no longer distinguish even the three characteristic shots of the German batteries in rafale fire. The noise was incessant, and each shell as it burst illumined a small section of the battlefield for a second. It just showed a tree trunk, a bit of wall, a strip of hedge, and then the darkness fell again over this point, while another was illuminated by the crash of a new explosion.

At one moment a sudden horror gripped me. To my left a shrapnel shell fell full on the line of the third squadron. This time the flash of the explosion had not only lighted up a corner of landscape; I had had a glimpse of a terrible sight.

You must imagine the intense and rapid light cast by a burning magnesium wire, accompanied by a deafening noise, and in this brief light the figures of several men, weirdly illuminated, in the attitudes induced by the terror of certain death, and you will get a faint impression of what I saw. Then, suddenly, everything fell back into darkness, a darkness that seemed more intense than before after the glare of the explosion. I dimly discerned bodies on the ground, and shadows bending over them.

I did not stop, but I heard the voice of the Major calmly giving orders:

"Pick him up! Gently...."

But the wounded man shrieked, refusing to allow himself to be touched; his limbs, no doubt, were shattered. No matter! Forward! Forward! We rushed on towards the wood, where we hoped to get some protection from the avalanche of shells. A voice called out names behind me:

"Corporal David killed! Sergeant Flosse wounded; leg broken."

My men were running forward so impetuously that presently they were on a level with me. What fine fellows! I half regretted that some hostile troop was not waiting for us ambushed in the wood. We might have had a splendid fight! But would there have been a fight at all? Would the Prussians have ventured to measure themselves against these dare-devils, whom danger excites instead of depressing? Well, we were at the edge of the wood at last, waiting till the Major came up with us.

Leaning against the trees, my Chasseurs took breath after their race. I passed swiftly along the line to make sure that all my men were safe. They were all there, and I was relieved to find that I had no losses to deplore. The joys and sorrows of war had forged a bond between us that nothing could break. I had soon learnt to know each one of them, with his virtues and his faults, and I felt them to be, without exception, worthy fellows and brave soldiers. Each time death struck down one of them, I suffered as at the loss of a beloved brother, and I believe they repaid my affection for them by perfect trust.

The Major had now rejoined us. We were not to lose a moment in responding to our Colonel's summons, and we were to remember that our comrades of the second squadron were bearing the brunt of the enemy's attack alone.

"Forward!"

We resumed our headlong advance. It was more difficult in the darkness of the wood than on the soft earth of the fields. We stumbled over roots, and got entangled in brambles; men fell, picked themselves up again, and went on with an oath. There was no more chaff; all minds were strung up to fever pitch, and strength was giving out, while the storm of shrapnel continued overhead, cropping the branches, and lighting up the tangle of leafless trees and bushes at intervals as if with fireworks.

Suddenly I heard on my right, not far behind me, screams and calls for help, rising above the turmoil of battle. I saw my men stop for a moment, looking round. But they hurried on again at my orders without a word.

"Forward!"

Time was precious. Every minute might be fatal to our brothers in arms. We could now hear the familiar sound of our cavalry carbines quite close to us. We were approaching the trenches where the second squadron was making its heroic stand.

"Forward! Forward!"

We were all breathless from our frantic rush. But no one thought of slackening speed. I turned round to some one who was trotting behind me. It was my non-commissioned officer. Without a moment's loss of time he had run to see what had caused the cries we had heard, and now he had come back at the double to report to me.

"Sir, in the third troop, Sergeant Lagaraldi...."

"Well?"

"He's killed, ... and Corporal Durand too!"

"Ah!"

"And there are many wounded."

I made no answer. Oh! it was horrible! Two poor fellows so full of life and spirits not an hour ago! In spite of myself I could not help thinking for a few minutes of the two shattered, quivering bodies lying among the grasses of the forest. But I thrust away the gruesome vision resolutely. We could only think of doing our duty at this supreme moment. Later we would remember the dead, weep for them, and pray for them.

The darkness was no longer so dense. The tangle of trees in front of us was less thick, the branches seemed to be opening out, we were near the edge of the wood. And at the same time, in spite of the mad beating of my heart and the buzzing in my ears, I was conscious that the cannonade had ceased, at least in our direction, and that the bullets were no longer coming so thickly. The German attack was probably relaxing; there was to be a respite. So much the better! It would enable us to pass from the wood to the trenches without much danger, thanks to the darkness.

We had arrived! One by one our men slipped into the communication trench. What a sense of well-being and of rest we all had! The little passage in the earth, so uninviting as a rule, seemed to us as desirable as the most sumptuous palace. We drew breath at last. We felt almost safe. But still, there was no time to be lost.

While the Major hurried off to take the Colonel's orders I climbed up on the parapet. Night had now fallen completely, but the moon was rising. Indeed, it would have been almost as light as day but for a slight mist which was spreading a diaphanous veil before our eyes. In the foreground to the right I could barely guess the dim outline of the battered mill and the burnt farm flanking the trench occupied by the foot Chasseurs. Further off, however, I could vaguely distinguish the row of trees that marked the first line of German trenches, about 250 yards away from us. To the left the mist had a reddish tinge. No doubt yet another house was burning in the unhappy village of Bixschoote.

There was a sudden silence in this little corner of the great battlefield, as if our arrival in the firing line had been a prearranged signal. On our right, too, the intensity of the fire upon the trenches occupied by the —— Territorials diminished. To the left, on the other hand, the gun fire and rifle fire were incessant in the direction of the bridge of Steenstraate, defended by the—Brigade of mounted Chasseurs. It seemed evident that the Germans, having failed in their attempt to cross the Yser canal near us, were making a fresh effort further to the north. However, it is not safe to rely too absolutely even upon the most logical deductions, for very often the event upsets the most careful calculations and frustrates the wisest plans.

The moon was now shining with extraordinary brilliance, and the fog, far from veiling its lustre, seemed to make it more disconcerting. Persons assumed strange forms and the shapes of things were modified or exaggerated. Our dazzled eyes were mocked by depressing hallucinations; the smallest objects took on alarming proportions, and whenever a slight breeze stirred the foliage of the beetroot field in front of us we imagined we saw a line of snipers advancing.

I had great difficulty in preventing my men from firing. It was necessary to eke out our cartridges with the utmost care, for, owing to some mistake in the transmission of orders, our supplies had not been replenished since the day before, and we had used a great many in the fighting round Bixschoote. A like prudence was not, however, observed all along the line, for every now and then the trenches would be suddenly illuminated at a point where for a few seconds a useless volley would ring out. Then everything relapsed into darkness and immobility.

Towards Steenstraate, too, the firing seemed to be dying down. I looked at my watch. It was half-past six. This was the hour when as a rule our men began to feel hungry, and when in each troop the Chasseurs would set out, pannikin in hand, towards the smoking saucepan where the cook awaited them wielding his ladle with an important air. But on this particular evening no one thought of eating. We seemed all to feel that our work was not yet over, and that we had still a weighty task on hand. It was certainly not the moment to light fires and make soup; no doubt the Prussians were brewing something for us of a different kind, and it would never do not to return their compliments promptly.

Ready? Yes, we were ready. I turned and looked back into the trench. All my brave fellows were standing, their eyes turned to me, and seemed bent on divining by my attitude or gestures any new effort I might be about to ask of them. The pale light of the moonbeams struck full on their faces, leaving their bodies shrouded in the darkness of the trench. What a strange and comforting spectacle it was! In every eye I read calm courage and absolute confidence.

Whenever I feel weary or depressed, inclined to curse the slowness of our advance and the thousand miseries of war, I need only do what I did that evening. I need only turn to my Chasseurs and look into their eyes without a word; there I read so many noble and touching things that I am ashamed to have felt a momentary weakness.

They do not ask the why and the wherefore of things. They live from day to day, weighed down by hard work. To them the actual fighting is a rest and a delight. As soon as it is over they have to resume the hard life of cavalrymen on active service, spend all their time looking after their horses, fetching rations and forage, often from a considerable distance, cleaning harness and arms, and every night contriving some sort of quarters for themselves and their beasts in the squalor of half-destroyed or abandoned villages, quarters they must leave on the morrow. Yet nothing seems to depress them. They preserve all the eagerness of the first few days and that imperishable French gaiety which is an additional weapon for our troops.

That evening I felt them vibrating in unison with me more keenly than ever.

There was little doubt that I should have to appeal to their courage again presently, for something unusual was happening in front of us. It was maddening not to be able to pierce the luminous mist, behind which the enemy would be able to form up and take new positions without our knowledge. Down behind the line of willows we could now barely distinguish, we were aware of mysterious sounds, making a kind of distant murmur. They must come from the rattle of arms, orders given in whispers, footsteps slipping on the fat soil of plough-lands. Listening heads craned over our parapets. Each man was trying to hear, to understand, to see, and to divine, and each felt intuitively that the enemy was about to renew his assault. The most absolute silence and the most impressive calm reigned in our trenches. Yes, we were ready for them! Let them come!

Then suddenly from the enemy's camp there rose a solemn, harmonious hymn sung by hundreds of manly voices. We could not distinguish the words uttered in the barbarian tongue. But the music was perfectly audible, and I must confess that nothing caused me so much surprise throughout this eventful evening. With what ardour and unanimity, and also, I am bound to admit, with what art, these men proclaimed their faith before rushing on death! One could imagine no more magnificent temple for the prayers of soldiers about to offer up their lives than the spacious firmament above and the luminous night around. We listened, touched and delighted. The hymn continued for some time, and the music seemed to me noble and inspiring; the voices were true and the execution admirable. But, above all, the singing conveyed a disturbing impression of disciplined and ordered piety. To what lengths these men carry their love of command and obedience!

Suddenly the hymn broke off abruptly in a formidable uproar, above which rose thousands of voices shouting:

"Hurrah! Hurrah! Cavalry! Cavalry!"

Then, dominating the tumult, we heard their trumpets sounding the short, monotonous notes of the Prussian charge.

I leaped back into the trench.

"Independent fire!"

The whole French line burst into a violent and deafening fusillade. Each man seemed full of blind rage, of an exasperated lust for destruction. I saw them take aim rapidly, press the trigger, and reload in feverish haste. I was deafened and bewildered by the terrible noise of the firing in the narrow confines of the trench. To our left, the machine-gun section of my friend F. kept up an infernal racket.

But the German line had suddenly dropped to the ground. I could barely distinguish a swarm of grey shadows running about in the fog. Then not a single dark figure was visible on the pale background of the tragic scene. How many of the bodies we could no longer make out must have been lying lifeless, and how horrible their proximity must have been to the living stretched side by side with them!

Our men had ceased firing of their own accord, and a strange silence had succeeded to the deafening din. What was about to happen? Would they dare to come on again? We hoped so with all our hearts, for we felt that if we could keep our men in hand, and prevent them from firing at random, the enemy could never get at us. But, above all, it was essential to economise our ammunition, for if we were short of cartridges, what resistance could we offer to a bayonet charge with our little carbines reduced to silence?

The Germans must have been severely shaken, for they seemed afraid to resume the attack. Nothing was moving in the bare plain that stretched before us. During this respite an order came from the officer in command, passing from mouth to mouth:

"Hand it on: No firing without the word of command."

Then silence fell on our trenches, heavy and complete as on the landscape before us. Suddenly, on the place where the enemy's riflemen had thrown themselves on the ground, we saw a slim shadow rise and stand. The man had got up quietly, as if no danger threatened him. And, in spite of everything, it was impossible not to admire the gallantry of his act. He stood motionless for a second, leaning on his sword or a stick; then he raised his arm slowly, and a hoarse voice yelled:

" Auf! " [Up!]

Other voices repeated the word of command, and were answered by renewed "hurrahs!" Then the heavy line of riflemen sprang up and again rushed towards us:

"Fire! Fire!"

Once more our trenches belched forth their infernal fire. We could now plainly see numbers of them fall; then they suddenly threw themselves on the ground just as before. But instead of crouching motionless among the beetroot they began to answer our fire. Innumerable bullets whistled about us. I noted with joy that my men remained perfectly steady; they were aiming and firing deliberately, whereas at other points the fusillade was so violent that it cannot have been efficacious. I was very glad not to have to reprove my brave Chasseurs, for the uproar was so terrific that my voice would not have carried beyond the two men nearest to me. I calculated the number of cartridges each of them must have in reserve; twenty-five, perhaps thirty. How would it all end? I was just thinking of ordering my troop to cease firing, in order to reserve my ammunition for a supreme effort, if this should be necessary.

But something happened which checked this decision. F.'s machine-guns must have worked fearful havoc among our assailants, for suddenly, without a cry and without an order, we saw them rise and make off quickly right and left in the fog.

"Silence!"

I was obliged to intervene to subdue the joyous effervescence caused in my troop. The men began to discuss their impressions in tones of glee that might have become dangerous. Ladoucette's voice was heard, as usual, above the din, calling upon his absent wife to admire his exploits:

"Madame Ladoucette, if you could have seen that!"

But we had to be on the qui vive .The German attack had been checked, but it might be renewed.

We were fully alive to the courage and tenacity of our enemies.

I could distinguish nothing ahead in the increasingly thick white fog. All I could hear was the sound of pickaxes on the ground and the thud of falling clods. The enemy had, no doubt, decided not to attack again and were digging new trenches. They no longer uttered their contemptuous guttural cries of "Cavalry! Cavalry!" They had learnt to their cost that these French cavalrymen, at the sight of whom their own are so ready to turn back, could hold their own equally well against German infantry. I thought we might count on a little respite. The battlefield was silent, save for the faint cries occasionally uttered by the wounded.

I hastily detached two troopers to man the listening-posts, and they slipped away silently. Then, as our Captain had unfortunately been summoned to Elverdinghe that day on special duty, I went to look for the Major to make my report to him. My men had seated themselves on the rough ledges cut in the slope of the trench, their carbines between their knees, and were talking together in low tones. As I passed a friendly smile lit up their faces. I walked slowly along the narrow trench, careful not to tread on the feet of the talkers.

As I approached a point where the trench, following the direction of the wood, formed an abrupt angle, I heard two familiar voices exchanging the following words:

"Fifty-two!... Tierce major...; three aces!" "Capital!"

This was really the limit! I turned the corner and came upon Major B. and F. seated on the ledge, quietly playing cards by the brilliant moonlight. As their tiny retreat could not accommodate four players, they were solacing themselves with a game of piquet.

Oh, all you who are of necessity far from the scene of conflict, good Frenchmen and valiant Frenchwomen, how I should have liked you to see this picture! No doubt you often wonder whether those who are defending your homes against the accursed invader will be able to bear the sufferings of this war to the bitter end; you fear that they may be losing their good humour and their dashing spirits; you imagine them brooding with careworn faces and anxious souls when, the excitement of the encounter dying down, they think of what the morrow may bring forth. How I wish you could have seen Major B. and the gallant Lieutenant F. playing piquet in the trench where they had just repulsed a furious German attack, which might have been renewed at any moment!

I left them to go on with their game, and went in search of my comrade O. I found him in the middle of his troop, talking amicably with his men. After the enemy had ceased firing he had sent a party of sappers to dig the graves of the two non-commissioned officers who had fallen in the wood. We retired into a corner of the trench, and there he told me of the grief he felt at this loss, a grief he was doing his best to hide, so as not to injure the moral of his troop. Lagaraldi had just got his promotion, and was a soldier of the highest promise; Durand was the model corporal, clean, cheerful, and active. And, even if they had been but mediocre troopers, I knew too well what we officers feel when we lose even a passable Chasseur, to wonder at the melancholy of my charming young comrade.

Time went on, and there were no signs of a fresh attack. The enemy's artillery seemed to be neglecting us, and to be bent upon the destruction of the Boesinghe bridge, by which we had crossed the Yser. His great shells flew over our heads with a sinister roar, and a few seconds later we heard the explosion far behind us. The German trenches in front of us were silent. A single shot fired at intervals alone reminded us that they were not forsaken.

" Mon Lieutenant, it's all ready."

A corporal had come out of the wood to tell O. that the graves were dug. When we had sent word to our chiefs, and placed our non-commissioned officers in temporary command, our strange, sad procession of mourners left the trenches and slipped through the thicket in single file. There were four officers, the Lieutenant-Colonel, Major B., O., and myself and four non-commissioned officers. It would have been dangerous to deplete the firing line further.

With heavy hearts we retraced our steps through the wood we had so lately passed through in all the exaltation of our advance. We knew the moral anguish we were about to feel in rendering this last service to our young brothers-in-arms. It was unhappily by no means the first time we had held such a ceremony, but never had I been present at one in such tragic circumstances, nor in such impressive surroundings. We hurried along, almost running in our anxiety to return quickly to our men. The branches caught at us and slashed our faces, the dead leaves and twigs crackled under our tread. Above us the shells still sang their funeral song.

We had now come in sight of the burial-ground. In the moonlight, at the edge of the wood close to the spot where our gallant fellows had fallen, we could distinguish newly-dug earth, and four silent men standing beside it, their tunics thrown off, leaning on spade and pickaxe. It was there.

In a little ravaged garden-plot, at the foot of great trees which would guard these graves, they had dug two holes, which, by night, looked extraordinarily deep and dark.

Ought we to lament or to envy the touching and simple burial rite of soldiers? To me, nothing could be more beautiful than such a last resting-place. Why should we desire richer tombs, sepulchral stones, and sculptured monuments? We are all equal upon that field of death, the battlefield at the close of day. And there can be no fitter shroud for him who has fallen on that field than his soldier's cloak. A little earth that will be grass-grown and flower-spangled again in the spring, a simple cross of rough wood, a name, a regimental number, a date—all this is better than the most splendid obsequies. And what can be more touching than the poor little bunches of wild flowers which the friends of the dead gather on the banks of ditches, and which are to be seen days afterwards, faded and yet so fair, hanging on the humble crosses? Such was to be the portion of Lagaraldi and Durand. Why should we pity them? We will weep for them, we will not pity them.

They were there, lying side by side in their cloaks, the turned-up capes of which shrouded their heads, and we bared our own in silence. Each of us, consciously or unconsciously, breathed a prayer, each set his teeth and tried to restrain his tears.

But we were not destined to pray in peace to the end. At the moment when the Lieutenant-Colonel was about to express our sorrow and pronounce the last farewell the enemy's mortars, suddenly changing their objective, began to bombard the part of the wood on the edge of which we were standing.

What was their idea? Did they think our reserves were massed in the wood? However this may have been, a formidable avalanche descended above and around us. The first salvo literally cleared the wood close by us. A great tree, cut through the middle, bent over for an instant and then rolled gently to the ground with a great crackling of broken boughs. At the same time the German bullets began to whistle round us by thousands, apparently determined to draw us into their frenzied saraband. Death seemed for a moment inevitable. We could not hesitate; we had to take cover, or to be mown down by shot or shell.

Then—I shall remember the gruesome moment to my dying hour—we all leaped into the only available shelter—crouching together in the newly-dug graves. We were just in time.

Bullets flew past us; the great "coal-boxes" burst without intermission. The uproar was tremendous, beyond anything we had ever heard. It would be impossible to describe the horror of those minutes. Those graves, all too spacious for the poor bodies we were about to commit to them, were too small to shelter us. We pressed one against the other in the strangest positions, hiding our heads between the shoulders of those who were lying in front of us; we thought every moment that the network of projectiles would be drawn more tightly round us, and that one would fall into our holes, transforming them into a ghastly charnel-house.

This idea occurred to me suddenly and obsessed me. Yes, yes, presently the great snorting, whistling, pitiless thing would fall between O. and me. We should feel nothing; there would be no pain. We should be only a little heap of bloody clay, and to-morrow at daybreak our comrades would but have to throw a few spadefuls of earth upon it. They would put a plain wooden cross above, with our names and ranks, the number of our regiment, a date: "November 3, 1914." And it would be better than any sumptuous monument.

"Hush! Listen!"

Between two explosions, in spite of the noise of the German bullets, we distinctly heard the crack of our carbines.

"Our men are fighting!"

We all understood, and with one bound we were up and running frantically through the wood. How was it that none of us were killed? How did we manage to escape the shells and bullets which were cropping the branches and felling the trees around us? I shall never understand or forget this experience.

When at last we sprang breathless into our trench after what had seemed an interminable race, the tumult had died down again and only occasional shots broke the nocturnal calm. The reason of the sudden renewal of the fighting was given at once by F.

"Bravo!" he cried; "we have retaken the infantry Chasseurs' trench!"

This was a great consolation to us, for we were all full of regret at the loss of this little piece of ground. It had prevented us from feeling quite satisfied with our day.

Now all was well. Our task was accomplished.

* * * * *

On the following day, November 4, at three in the morning, a battalion of the —— Regiment of the Line came to relieve us. It formed part of that glorious 20th Corps, which has covered itself with glory ever since the beginning of the war, and fought all along the front from Lorraine to Flanders, always arriving at the moment when picked men were needed to make a last desperate effort. It had come up that evening, and was at once on the spot.

In the cold, luminous night, the heavily laden infantrymen defiled into the narrow trench, calm, silent, and serious.

The officer who was to take my place presented himself smartly, as if on the parade-ground.

"Lieutenant X."

I gave my name.

"My dear fellow," he said, "I am delighted to shake hands with you. Allow me to say how much we all admire your regiment. Your General has just told us how your Chasseurs have behaved. Accept my congratulations. We could not have done better ourselves. The cavalry is certainly taking first place as a fighting force. Your regiment is to be mentioned in despatches, and you deserve it. Good-night. Good luck!"

"Thank you! Good luck!"

* * * * *

Once more we passed through the wood to take up our position in reserve. Our men were beginning to feel the fatigue of those two days without sleep and almost without rest.

But joy, stronger than bodily fatigue, predominated. It hovered over our harassed troops. Above all, they were proud of having been appreciated and congratulated by their brothers-in-arms of the crack corps which is the admiration of the whole army.

Each man forgot his tortured nerves, his aching head, his weary legs, repeating to himself the magic words:

"Your regiment is to be mentioned in despatches!"

Chapter 7
SISTER GABRIELLE

It was a very dark night. How were we to find our way about the little unknown town of Elverdinghe, near which our regiment had just been quartered? We could hardly make out the low houses with closed windows and long roofs of thatch or slate, and kept stumbling on the greasy and uneven cobble-stones. Now and again the corner of a street or the angle of a square was lit up dimly by a ray of light filtering through half-closed shutters. I went along haphazard, preceded by my friend B. We were quite determined to find beds, and to sleep in peace.

After our four days' fighting near Bixschoote we had been sent to the rear, ten kilometres away from the line of fire, to get twenty-four hours' rest; had arrived at nightfall, and found much difficulty in putting up our men and horses in the small farms around the town. But no sooner had they all found places, no sooner had the horses got their nose-bags on and the kitchen fires been lighted, than B., who was always anxious about the comforts of his board and lodging, said to me:

"There is only one thing for us to do. We are to rest. We must find a bed and a well-furnished table. I had rather go to bed an hour later, and sleep between sheets after a good meal, than lie down at once on straw with an empty stomach. Listen to me. Let us go on to that nice Belgian town over there, only a few steps farther. It is hardly ten o'clock.

It will be devilish bad luck if we can't find a good supper and good quarters. We need not trouble about anything else. Let us think first of serious matters."

So we started for the little town which seemed to be wrapped in sleep. We knocked at the doors, but not one opened; no doubt the houses were all full of soldiers. No one offered us any hospitality, in spite of all B.'s objurgations, now beseeching, now imperious. In despair, I suggested at last that we should go back to our squadron, and lie down by our horses; but B. would not hear of it, and still clung to his idea: to have a good dinner, and sleep in a bed.

Just then, we saw a dark figure creeping noiselessly along under the wall. B. at once went up to it, and caught it by the arm. It was a poor old woman, carrying a basket and a jug of milk. Said he:

"Madame, madame, have pity on two poor weary, half-starved soldiers...."

But she couldn't give us any information. Speaking in bad French, interspersed with Flemish, she gave us to understand that the little town was full of troops, and, at that hour, everybody was asleep.

"And what is there in that large white building, where the windows are alight?"

The good woman explained that it was a convent, where nuns took in the old people of the country. They could not give lodging to soldiers. But B. had already made up his mind; that was where we were to sleep. Leaving the old woman aghast, he went with long strides to the iron railing which surrounded a little garden in front of the convent. I tried in vain to make him understand that we could not invade these sacred precincts.

"Leave it to me," he said, "I'll speak to them."

He pushed the iron gate, which opened with a creak, and I shut it after him. I felt somewhat uneasy as I followed B., who crossed the garden with a rapid stride. I felt uneasy at the thought of his essentially military eloquence, and of the use to which he proposed to put it. But I knew, too, that he was not easily induced to abandon a resolution he had once taken. True, he did not often make one, but this time he seemed to be carrying out a very definite plan. The best thing was to submit, and await the result of his attempt. We went up three steps, and felt for the knocker. "Here it is," said B., and he lifted it and knocked hard. What a dismal sound it made in that sleeping town! I felt as though we had just committed an act of sacrilege. We listened, and heard, through the door, the noise of chairs dragged over the stone floor; then a light footstep approaching, a sound of keys and bolts, and the door was gently opened and held ajar.

"Sister," said B., with a bow, "what we are doing is, I know, most unusual; but we are dying of hunger and very tired, and, so far, nobody has been willing to open their door to us. Could we not have something to eat here, and sleep in a bed?"

The Sister looked at us and appeared not to understand. However, I was more at ease when I saw she was neither frightened nor displeased. She was a very old nun, dressed in black, and held in her hand a little lamp which flickered in the night breeze. Her face was furrowed with deep wrinkles, and her skinny hand, held before the lamp, seemed transparent. She made up her mind at once. Her face lit up with a kind smile, and she signed to us to come in, with words which were probably friendly. This was a supposition, for the worthy nun only spoke Flemish, and we could not understand anything she said. She carefully pushed the bolts again, placed her lamp on the floor, and made a sign to us to wait. Then she went away with noiseless steps, and we were left alone.

"You see," said B., "it is all going swimmingly. Now that we have got in, you must leave everything to me."

The flickering lamp lighted the hall dimly. The walls were bare, and there was no furniture but some rush chairs set in a line against the partition. Opposite the door, there was a simple wooden crucifix, and the stretched-out arms seemed to bid us welcome. A perfume of hot soup came from the door the old Sister had just shut.

"I say!" said B., "did you smell it? I believe it is cabbage soup, and if so, I shall take a second helping."

"Just wait a bit," I replied; "I'll wager they are going to turn us out."

From the other side of the door, by which the portress had just disappeared, we heard a voice calling:

"Sister Gabrielle!... Sister Gabrielle!..."

And a moment after, the same door opened, and another nun came in very quietly, and rather embarrassed, as it seemed to me. She came towards us.

Sister Gabrielle, your modesty will certainly suffer from all the good I am going to say of you.... But I am wrong, you will not suffer, for you certainly will never read the pages I have scribbled during the course of this war, at odd times, as I could, in bivouacs and billets. But I have vowed to keep a written record of the pictures which have charmed or moved me most during this campaign. If I ever survive it, I want to be able to read them again in my latter days. I want to have them read by those who belong to me, and to try to show them what kind of life we led during those unforgettable days. And it is not always the battles which leave the most lively impressions. How many delightful things one could relate that have happened outside the sphere of action! What memories of nights passed in the strangest places, as the chances of the march decreed, nights of bitterness during the retreat, nights of fever during the advance, nights of depression in the trenches! What kindly welcomes, what beautiful and what noble figures one might describe!

Sister Gabrielle, as you will never read this, and as your modesty will not suffer, let me tell the story of the welcome my friend B. and I received that evening at the Convent of Elverdinghe.

Sister Gabrielle came towards us. How pretty she was, in the coif that framed her face! How large her blue eyes looked! They really were so, but a touch of excitement made them seem larger still. Above all, she had an enchanting smile, a smile of such kindness that we at once felt at ease and sure of obtaining what we wanted. She spoke in a sweet and musical voice, hesitating just a little in her choice of words, although she spoke French very correctly.

"The Sister Superior has sent me to you," she said, "because I am the only one here who can speak French.... Messieurs les officiers, welcome."

She said it quite simply, and stood quite straight in her black dress, her arms hanging beside her. She might have been a picture of other days, an illuminated figure from a missal. We looked at each other and smiled too, happy to find so unexpected a welcome. B. was now quite self-possessed.

"Sister Gabrielle," he said, "see what a wretched state we are in; our clothes covered with mud, our faces not washed since I don't know when. We have just gone four days without sleep, almost without food, and we have never stopped fighting. Could you not take in two weary, famished soldiers for one night?"

Sister Gabrielle retained her wonderful smile. Without moving her arms, she slightly raised her two hands, which showed white against the black cloth of her dress. Those hands seemed to say: "I should like to very much, but I cannot." And at the same time the smile said: "We ought not to, but it shall be managed nevertheless."

"Come," she said; "in any case, we can give you something to eat."

And she took up the little lamp. She went first, opened the door at the end of the passage, and we followed her, delighted. We were dazzled as we came into this new room by the brilliance of the lamps that lit it. It was the convent kitchen. How clean and bright everything was! The copper saucepans shone resplendently. The black and white pavement looked like an ivory chessboard. Two Sisters were sitting peeling vegetables which they threw into a bowl of water. An enormous pot, on the well-polished stove, was humming its inviting monotone. It was this pot which exhaled the delicious smell that had greeted us when we entered the house. The whole picture recalled one of Bail's appetising canvases. The two Sisters raised their eyes, looked at us and—yes, they smiled too. B., feeling eloquent, wanted to make a speech; but Sister Gabrielle hurried us on:

"Come, come," she said. "It is not worth while; they wouldn't understand you."

She opened another door, and we went into a small rectangular room. Whilst our guide hastened to light the lamp hanging above the table, we laid our kits on the window-sill: our revolvers, shakoes, binocular glasses and map-cases; and how tarnished and dirty the things were, after those three months of war! We ourselves felt fairly ashamed to be seen in such a state. Our coats worn and stained, our breeches patched, our huge boots covered with mud, all formed a strange contrast to the room we were in. It was provided throughout with large cupboards in the walls, the doors of which reached to the ceiling. These doors were of polished wood, and shone like a mirror. The floor was like another mirror. That indefatigable chatterer B. began another speech:

"Sister, please excuse the costumes of fighting men. We

must look like ruffians, but we are honest folk. If our faces do not inspire much confidence, it is simply because our stomachs are so empty. And no one more resembles a vagabond than a poor wretch who is dying with hunger. You will not know us again after we have had a few words with the pot which gave out such a savoury smell as we passed."

Sister Gabrielle did not cease to smile. With wonderful rapidity and skill she opened one of the cupboards, and, from the piles of linen, picked out a checkered red and white tablecloth with which she covered the table. In a moment she had arranged places for two, opposite each other.

"Sit down," she said, "and rest. I will go and fetch you something to eat."

B. followed her to the door.

"Sister Gabrielle," he said, "we have found a Paradise."

But she had already shut the door, and we heard her in the kitchen stimulating the zeal of the other two nuns in Flemish. We sat down, delighted. What a long time since we had enjoyed such comfort! Everything there seemed designed to charm our eyes and rest our minds. There was no noise in the street, and the convent itself would have seemed wrapped in sleep had it not been for the voices in the next room. But the distant roar of the guns still went on, and seemed to make our respite still more enjoyable.

We hardly heard Sister Gabrielle when she came in and put down the steaming soup before us. The delicate perfume of the vegetables made our mouths water. For many days past we had had nothing to eat but our rations of tinned meat, and all that time we had not been able to light a fire to cook anything at all. So we fell to eagerly upon our well-filled plates. B. even lost the power of speech for the moment.

Meanwhile the pretty little Sister, without appearing to look at us, was cutting bread, and then she brought a jug of golden beer. What a treat it was! Why couldn't it be like this every day? In that case the campaign would have seemed almost like a picnic. Whilst I was eating I could not help admiring Sister Gabrielle; she looked so refined in her modest black clothes. Her slightest movements were as harmonious as those of an actress on the stage. But she was natural in all she did, and the grace of every movement was instinctive. As she placed before us an imposing-looking omelette au lard, that rascal B., who had already swallowed two plates of soup and four large glasses of beer, began to maunder thus:

"Sister Gabrielle, ... Sister Gabrielle, I don't want to go away to-morrow. I want to end my days here with the old people you look after. Look at me. I am getting old too, and have been severely tried by life. Why shouldn't I stay where I am? I should have a nice little bed in the old people's dormitory, with nice white sheets, go to bed every evening on the stroke of eight, and you, Sister, would come and tuck me up. I should sleep, and eat cabbage soup, and drink good beer—your health. Sister!—and I shouldn't think any more about anything at all.... How nice it would be! No more uniform to strap you up after a good dinner; no more shako to squeeze your temples; no more bullets whistling past you; no more 'coal-boxes' to upset your whole system, and every evening a bed, ... a nice bed, ... and to think about nothing!..."

"Hush! Listen," said Sister Gabrielle with a finger on her lips.

At that moment the noise of the firing became louder. The Germans had no doubt just made a night attack either on Bixschoote or on Steenstraate, and now every piece was firing rapidly all along the line. So fast did the reports follow one another that they sounded like a continuous growl.

However, the noise seemed to be dominated by the reports that came from a battery of heavy guns ("long 120's") two kilometres from Elverdinghe, which made all the windows of the convent rattle, I shuddered as I thought of those thousands of shells, hurtling through the darkness for miles to reduce so many living human beings to poor broken and bleeding things. And I pictured to myself our Prussians of Bixschoote sprawling on the ground, with their teeth set and their heads hidden among the beetroot, waiting until the hurricane had passed, to get up again and rush forward with their bayonets, cheering! Sister Gabrielle had the same thought, no doubt. She looked still whiter than before under her white coif, and clasping her hands and lowering her eyes, she said in a low voice:

"Mon Dieu, ... Mon Dieu! ... It is horrible!"

"Sister Gabrielle," continued the incorrigible B., "don't let us talk of such things. Let us rather discuss this omelette, a dish worthy of the gods, and the bacon in it, the savour of which might imperil a saint. Sister Gabrielle, you tempt us this evening to commit the sin of gluttony, which is the most venial of all sins. And I will bear the burden of it manfully."

I kicked B. under the table, to stop his incongruous remarks. But Sister Gabrielle seemed not to have listened to him. She went on serving us smilingly; changed our plates, and brought us ham and cheese. B. went on devouring everything that was put before him; but this did not put a stop to his divagations.

"Tell me, Sister Gabrielle, you are not going to turn us out of the house now, are you? It would be an offence against God, who commands us to pity travellers. And we are poor wretched travellers. If you drive us away, we shall have to sleep on the grass by the roadside, with stones for our pillows. No, you couldn't treat us so cruelly. I feel sure that in a few minutes you will show me the bed in the dormitory you will keep for me when I come to take up my quarters with you after the war."

Sister Gabrielle's smile had disappeared. For the first time, she seemed really distressed. She stopped in front of B., and looked at him with her large clear eyes. She made the same gesture as before; lifted up both her hands, in token of powerlessness, and seemed to be thinking how she could avoid hurting our feelings. Then she said, in a disheartened tone:

"But we have not a single spare bed."

A long silence followed this sentence, which seemed to plunge B. into despair. The guns continued their ominous booming, making the windows rattle terribly. I too thought now that it would be dreadful to leave the house, go and look for our troops in the dark, and put our men to the inconvenience of making room for us on their straw, so I too looked at Sister Gabrielle imploringly. All at once she seemed to have decided what to do. She began by opening one of the cupboards in the wall, took out of it two small glasses with long tapering stems, and placed them before us, with a goodly bottle of Hollands. She had recovered her exquisite smile, and she hurried, for she seemed anxious to put her idea into execution.

"There, drink. It's good Hollands, ... and we give it to our poor old people on festivals."

"Thank you. Sister, thank you."

But she had already run out of the room, and we were left there, happy enough, sipping our glass of Hollands, and enjoying the luxurious peace that surrounded us. The guns seemed to be further off; we only heard a distant growling in the direction of Yprès. Our eyelids began to droop, and it was almost a pleasure to feel the weariness of our limbs and heads, for now we felt sure that Sister Gabrielle would not send us away.

She came back into the room, with a candle in her hand.

"Come," she said.

She was now quite rosy, and seemed ashamed, as though she were committing a fault. We followed her, enchanted, and went back through the kitchen, now dark and deserted. The flickering light of the candle was reflected here and there on the curves of the copper pots and glass bowls. The house was sleeping. We crossed the hall, and went up a broad wooden staircase, polished and shining.

What a strange party we were, the youthful Sister, going in front, treading so softly, and we two soldiers, dusty, tattered and squalid, trying to make as little noise as possible with our heavy hobnailed boots! The nun's rosary clinked at each step against a bundle of keys that hung from her girdle.

I was walking last and enjoying the curious picture. The light fell only on Sister Gabrielle. As she turned on the landing, the feeble ray from below threw her delicate features into relief: her fine nose, her childish mouth, with its constant smile; our own shadows appeared upon the wall in fantastic shapes. Certainly we had never yet received so strange and unexpected a welcome.

We passed a high oak door, surmounted by a cross and a pediment with a Latin inscription. Sister Gabrielle crossed herself and bowed her head.

"The chapel," she said in a low voice.

And she went quickly on to the accompaniment of her clinking rosary and keys. As we began to go up the second flight of stairs B. resumed his monologue in a whisper:

"Sister Gabrielle, ... Sister Gabrielle, you are an angel from Paradise. Surely God can refuse you nothing. You will pray for me this evening, won't you? for I am a great sinner."

"Oh, yes, of course I shall pray for you," she answered, softly, as she turned towards us.

We came out on a long passage, bare and whitewashed. Half a dozen doors could be distinguished at regular intervals, all alike. Sister Gabrielle opened one of them, and we followed her in. We found ourselves in a small room, austerely furnished with two little iron bedsteads, two little deal tables, and two rush chairs. Above each bed there was a crucifix, with a branch of box attached to it. Each table had a tiny white basin and a tiny water-jug. All this was very nice, and amply sufficient for us. Everything was clean, bright, and polished.

"Thank you, Sister; we shall be as comfortable as possible. But, one thing, we shall sleep like tops. Will there be any one to wake us?"

"At what time do you want to get up?"

"At six, Sister, punctually, as soldiers must, you know."

"Oh! then I will see to it. We have Mass at four o'clock every morning."

"At four o'clock!" exclaimed B. "Every morning! Very well, Sister, to show you we are not miscreants, wake us at half-past three, and we will go to Mass too."

"But it isn't allowed. It is our Mass, in our chapel. No, no, you must sleep.... Get to bed quickly. Good-night. I will wake you at six o'clock."

"Good-night, Sister Gabrielle; good-night.... We shall be so comfortable. You see, you had some spare beds, after all."

"Oh, yes, we had. One can always manage somehow."

And she went off, shutting the door behind her.

And now B. and I thought of nothing but the luxury of sleeping in a bed. How delightful it would be after our sleepless nights in the fogs of the trenches!

But what was that noise resounding through the convent? What was that knocking and those wailing cries? There was some one at the door, hammering at the knocker, some one weeping and sobbing in the dark. I opened my window, and leant out. But the front door had already been opened, and a figure slipped in hurriedly. The sobs came up the stairs to our door, and women's voices, Sister Gabrielle's voice, speaking Flemish, then another voice, sounding like a death-rattle, trying in vain to pronounce words through choking sobs. How horrible that monotonous, inconsolable, continual wail was! It went on for a short time, and then doors were opened and shut, the voices died away, and suddenly the noise ceased.

B. had already got into bed, and, from under the sheets, he begged me, in a voice muffled by the bed-clothes, to put the candle out quickly. But I was haunted by that moaning, though I could not hear it any longer. I wanted to know what tragedy had caused those sobs. I could not doubt that the horrible war was at the bottom of it. And yet we were a long way from the firing line. My curiosity overcame my fatigue. I put on my jacket and went out, taking the candle with me. I ran down the two staircases, and my footsteps seemed to wake dismal echoes in the silent convent.

Just as I came to the hall Sister Gabrielle also arrived, with a small lantern in her hand. I must have frightened her, for she started and gave a little scream. But she soon recovered, and guessed what had disturbed me. She told me all about it in a few simple sentences; a poor woman had fled from her village, carrying her little girl of eighteen months. As she was running distractedly along the road from Lizerne to Boesinghe a German shell had fallen, and a fragment of it had killed her baby in her arms. She had just come six kilometres in the dark, clasping the little corpse to her breast in an agony of despair. She got to Elverdinghe, and knocked at the door of the convent, knowing that there she would find a refuge. And all along the road she had passed convoys, relief troops and despatch-riders; but she took no heed of them; she was obsessed by one thought; to find a shelter for the remains of what had been the joy and hope of her life.

"Just come," said Sister Gabrielle. "I will let you see her. We have put the poor little body in the mortuary chamber, and Sister Elizabeth is watching there."

I followed Sister Gabrielle, who opened a small door, and went down a few steps; we crossed a paved court. Her lantern and my candle cast yellowish gleams upon the high walls of the buildings. Heavy drops of rain were falling, making a strange noise on the stones. And a kind of anguish seized me when I again heard the continuous wailing of the unhappy mother. Sister Gabrielle opened a low door very gently, and we went in.

I must confess that I had been much less moved when, after the first day of the Battle of the Marne, we passed through a wood where our artillery had reduced a whole German regiment to a shapeless mass of human fragments. Here I realised all the horror of war. That men should kill each other in defence of their homes is conceivable enough, and I honour those who fall. But it passes all understanding why the massacre should include these poor weak and innocent creatures. And sights such as the one I saw in that little mortuary chapel inspire a fierce thirst for vengeance.

On a kind of large table, covered with a white cloth, the poor body was laid out. It bore no trace of any wound, and the little white face seemed to be smiling. The good nuns had covered the shabby clothes with an embroidered cloth. Upon that they had crossed the little hands, which seemed to be clasping a tiny crucifix. And over the whole they had strewn an armful of flowers. On each side they had placed silver candlesticks, and the reddish candle-light made golden reflections in the curly locks of the little corpse. Crouching on the ground by the side of it, I saw a shapeless heap of clothes which seemed to be shaken by convulsive spasms.

It was from this heap that the monotonous wailing came. It was the young mother, weeping for her little one. One felt that nothing could console her, and that words would only increase her suffering. Besides, she had not even raised her head when we went in. It was best to leave her alone, since they say that tears bring comfort.

On the other side a young Sister was kneeling at a prie-Dieu, telling her rosary. Sister Gabrielle knelt down on the ground beside her. I longed to do something to lessen that grief, and help the poor woman a little. She must have come there in a state of destitution: her clothes revealed her poverty. But I durst not disturb either her mourning or their prayers, and I came out quietly on tiptoe.

Outside, the rain, which was now falling heavily, refreshed my fevered head somewhat. I crossed the courtyard quickly; but my candle went out, and I had some trouble in relighting it, which was very necessary, as I had to find my way in a maze of doors and passages. At last I reached my staircase, and passed the landing and the Sisters' chapel. I heard a distant clock strike midnight, went up another storey, and opened our door noiselessly. I thought that B. would perhaps be waiting for me impatiently, anxious to learn the reason of all the noise.

But B. was snoring with the bed-clothes over his ears.

At six o'clock some one knocked at our door, and I opened my eyes. Daylight showed faintly through the only window. I wondered where I was, and suddenly remembered ... Elverdinghe ... the convent....

"Is it you, Sister Gabrielle?" I asked.

"Oh, yes, it's I. Get up. I have been knocking for more than an hour."

B. sat up in his bed. I did the same, and told him what I had seen the evening before. He shook his head mournfully, and concluded:

"Well, ... it's war.... I hope they'll have a good breakfast ready for us."

We hurried through our dressing and ablutions, for we had to get back quickly to our quarters. As we came out of our room, lively and refreshed, we met Sister Gabrielle, who seemed to have been waiting for us. She asked us how we had slept, and, to stop the flood of eloquence that B. was on the point of letting loose, she said:

"That's right. You shall thank me later on. Come down now; your breakfast is waiting for you. It will get cold."

But, on passing the chapel, B. would insist on seeing it. Sister Gabrielle hesitated a moment, and then gave way, as you would to a child for the sake of peace. She opened the outer door, and smiled indulgently, as if anxious to humour all our whims. We passed through an anteroom, and then entered the chapel. It was quite small, only large enough to hold about twenty people. The walls were white, without any ornament, and panelled up to about the height of a man. The altar was extremely simple, and decorated with a few flowers. Some rush chairs completed the plenishings of the sanctuary where the good Sisters of Elverdinghe assembled every morning at four o'clock for prayers.

And, as we came out of this humble chapel, I noticed two mattresses, laid in a corner of the little anteroom.

"Who sleeps here, then, Sister?" I asked.

Sister Gabrielle turned as red as a poppy. I had to repeat my question twice, when, lowering her eyes, she answered:

"Sister Elizabeth—Sister Elizabeth ... and I."

"Sister Gabrielle, ... Sister Gabrielle, then that little room and those two little beds where we slept, were yours?"

"Hush! Please come to breakfast at once."

And, light as a bird, she disappeared down the staircase, so quickly that her black veil floated high above her, as though to hide her confusion.

* * * * *

And we saw no more of Sister Gabrielle. It was a very old woman—one of the inmates—who brought us our hot milk and coffee, our brown bread and fresh butter, in the dining-room with the high cupboards of polished wood. She explained that at this hour the nuns were busy attending to their old folk. It was of no use begging to see our little hostess again. We were told it would be against the rules, and we felt that the curtain had now indeed fallen upon this charming act of the weary tragedy.

Only, just as we were passing out of the convent gate for the last time, the old lady put into our hands a big packet of provisions wrapped up in a napkin. She had brought it hidden under her apron.

"Here, she told me to give you this, and ... to say that she will pray for you."

Our hearts swelled as we heard the heavy door close behind us. And whilst we went away silently along the broken, muddy road, we thought of the sterling hearts that are hidden under the humble habits of a convent.

Sister Gabrielle! I shall never forget you. Never will your delicate features fade from my memory. And I seem to see you still, going up the great wooden staircase, lit up by the flickering flame of the candle, when you and Sister Elizabeth gave up your beds so simply and unostentatiously to the two unknown soldiers.

Chapter 8
Christmas Night

"Mon Lieutenant mon Lieutenant, it's two o'clock."

My faithful Wattrelot held the flickering candle just in front of my eyes to rouse me. What torture it is to be snatched from sleep at such an early hour! It would not be anything in summer; but it was the 24th of December, and it was my turn to go on duty in the trenches. A nice way of keeping Christmas!... I turned over in my bed, trying to avoid that light that tormented me; I collected my thoughts, which had wandered far away whilst I was asleep, and had been replaced by exquisite dreams, dreams of times of peace, of welfare, of good cheer, and of gentle warmth.

Then I remembered: I had to take command of a detachment of a hundred troopers of the regiment, who were to replace the hundred now in the trenches. It was nearly a month since we had joined our Army Corps near R., and every other day the regiment had to furnish the same number of men to occupy a sector of the trenches. It was my turn, on the 24th of December, to replace my brother-officer and good friend Lieutenant de la G., who had occupied the post since the 22nd.

I had forgotten all this.... How cold it was! Brrr!...

Whilst Wattrelot was taking himself off I braced myself for the necessary effort of getting out of the warm sheets. Like a coward, I kept on allowing myself successive respites, vowing to rise heroically after each.

"I will get up as soon as Wattrelot has reached the landing of the first floor.... I will get up when I hear him walking on the pavement of the hall, ... or rather when I hear the entrance-door shut, and his boots creaking on the gravel path...."

But every noise was hushed. Wattrelot was already some way off, and I still shied at this act, which, after all, was inevitable: to get out of bed in a little ice-cold room at two o'clock in the morning. Through the window, which had neither shutter nor curtain, I saw a small piece of the sky, beautifully clear, in which myriads of stars were twinkling. The day before, when I came in to go to bed, it was freezing hard. That morning the frost, I thought, must be terrible.

"Come, up!" With a bound I was on the ground, and rushed at once to the little pitch-pine washstand. Rapid ablutions would wake me up thoroughly. Horror! The water in the jug was frozen. Oh! not very deeply, no doubt; but all the same I had to break a coating of ice that had formed on the surface. However, I was happy to feel more nimble after having washed my face. Quick! Two warm waistcoats under my jacket, my large cloak with its cape, my fur gloves, my campaigning cap pulled over my ears, and there I was, with a candle in my hand, going down the grand staircase of the château.

For I was quartered in a château. The very word makes one think of a warm room, well upholstered, well furnished, with soft carpets and comfortable armchairs. But, alas! it was nothing of the sort.... The good lady whose house it was had provided for all contingencies; the family rooms had been prudently dismantled and double-locked. A formidable concierge had the keys, and I was happy indeed when I found the butler's room in the attics. His bed, with its white sheets, seemed to me very desirable. And then, as we say in time of peace, one must take things as they come.

The open hall-door let in a wave of cold air, which struck cold on my face. But I had not a minute to lose. The detachment was to start at half-past two punctually, and it had, no doubt, already formed up in the market-place. I hurried into the street. The tall pines of the park stood out black against the silver sky, whilst the bare branches of the other trees formed thousands of arabesques and strange patterns all round. Not the slightest noise was to be heard in the limpid, diaphanous night, in which the air seemed as pure and rare as on the summits of lofty mountains. Under my footsteps the gravel felt soft, but, once I had got outside the iron gate, I found myself on ground as hard as stone. The mud formed by recent rains and the ruts hollowed by streams of convoys had frozen, and the road was a maze of furrows and inequalities which made me stumble again and again.

In front of the Hôtel des Lacs a certain number of the men had already lined up, in front of their horses. Huddled in their cloaks, with collars turned up, they were stamping their feet and blowing into their hands. It must have been real torture for them too to come out of their straw litter, where they were sleeping so snugly a few moments before, rolled up in their blankets. They had got a liking for the kind of comfort peculiar to the campaigner, and had invented a thousand and one ingenious methods of improving the arrangements of their novel garrison. Sleeping parties had been gradually organised, and sets of seven or eight at a time enjoyed delightful nights, stretched on their clean straw. Many of them would certainly not be able to get to sleep if they suddenly found themselves in a real bed. And then it is less difficult to get up when one has gone to bed with one's clothes on, and when the room is not very warm. Not one of them complained; not one of them grumbled. We can always count on our brave fellows.

"All present, mon Lieutenant! "

It was the senior non-commissioned officers of the two squadrons assembled there who reported. Every one had got up and equipped himself at the appointed hour; not one was missing at roll-call; they had all assembled of their own accord; the corporals had not needed to knock at door after door to wake the sleepers. Our Chasseurs had very quickly established simple customs and rules of their own which ensured the regularity of the service without written orders. This intelligent and spontaneous discipline is one of the most admirable features of this campaign. It has grown up by degrees, without any special orders or prescriptions from above, with the result that the hardest labours are carried out almost without supervision, because each man understands the end in view and the grim necessities which it involves.

They understood at once that this early hour was the only one at which the relief could be effected. And every other day, just as on that December morning, twenty-five men out of each squadron get up at half-past one, equip themselves, and saddle their horses, whilst the cooks warm up a good cup of coffee for each man. Then, without any hurry, but at the exact moment, they form up in fighting order at the appointed spot, and when the officer arrives, in the dark, rain, wind, snow, or frost, he is sure of receiving the same report:

"All present, mon Lieutenant! "

Quick! Mount. We shall feel the cold less trotting over the hardened roads this bright night and under this brilliant moon. Two and two, in silence, we issued from the village in the direction of R. I knew that I should find a little further on, at the cross-roads where the crucifix stands, the fifty men of the first half-regiment and Second-Lieutenant de G., who serves under me.

Yes, there he was, coming to meet me on the hard road.

It was a joy to me that chance had given me this jolly fellow for my trench companion. I hardly knew him, for he had not been with us more than a few days. Taken from the Military College directly war was declared, he had first been sent to a reserve squadron, and had only just been appointed to an active regiment. But I already knew, through my comrades of the first squadron, that he was a daring soldier and a merry companion. So much the better, I thought. War is a sad thing, and one must learn to take it gaily. A plague on gloomy spirits and long faces! True, we can no longer wage the picturesque war of the "good old days." We shall never know another Fontenoy, or Rivoli, or Eylau. But that is no reason why we should lose the jovial humour of our forefathers. Thank Heaven! we have preserved their qualities of dash and bravery. But it is more difficult to keep a smiling face in this hideous mole warfare, which is imposed even upon us troopers. All the more reason for liking and admiring the cheery officers who keep our spirits up, and G. is one of them.

We shook hands without speaking, for it seemed to us that if we opened our mouths the frost would get into our bodies and freeze them, and we set off at a sharp trot along the narrow by-road which, crossing the high-road to Paris, leads to C. There we should have to leave our horses, cross the zone of the enemy's artillery fire, and get to the trenches on foot. The horses snorted with pleasure, happy to warm themselves by rapid movement. Some of them indulged in merry capers, which were repressed, not too gently, by their more sedate riders. Their hoofs struck the uneven ground with a metallic ring which must have echoed far; and the clink of bits and stirrups also disturbed the sleeping country. Before us the road ran straight amidst the dark fields, a long pale grey ribbon. No one thought of laughing or talking; sleep seemed still to hover over the column, and every one knew that the two days of trench duty would be long and hard to get through even if the Prussians left us in peace.

We passed a cross, which shone white on the side of the road under the pale light of the moon, and saluted it. We had known it from the first days, and had its inscription by heart:

80 NON-COMMISSIONED OFFICERS,
CORPORALS AND SOLDIERS OF THE
39TH AND 74TH REGIMENTS OF INFANTRY
KILLED IN ACTION.

PRAY FOR THEM.

We dimly discerned the modest wreaths of green leaves, now faded and yellow, and the little nosegays of withered flowers attached to the arms of this cross, left there after the departure of the regiment and undisturbed by any sacrilegious hand.

We crossed the Paris road, with its double row of trees, which, in the night, appeared gigantic, and, after answering the challenge of the Territorial guarding the approach to C., we entered the village.

It appeared to be completely empty, and yet there were two battalions of the—Territorials quartered there. The moon seemed to be amusing itself by casting the shadows of the houses on one side of the street upon the walls of the other side in fantastic shapes.

"Dismount."

We had reached the spot where we were to leave our horses. The men quickly unbuckled the blankets which were to help them to endure the weary hours of the following night. They slung them over their shoulders, and we set off towards the towing-path of the canal. We went very slowly, as we had at least seven or eight kilometres before us, and a walk of eight kilometres for troopers laden and dressed as we were is no light matter.

We found the towing-path. Walking at that hour of the night is certainly not very alluring. However, thc view was not lacking in grandeur. On either side of the canal the dark silhouettes of tall trees stood out against the sky. Their shadows were reflected in the water, which gleamed with a metallic lustre in the moonshine. How calm and silent it was! Who would have thought we were at war? Not a cannon-shot, not a rifle-shot, disturbed the peace of the night. Yet, as a rule, there were no long intervals between the reports which reminded us of the serious work on hand.

That day it seemed as though some agreement had been come to by both sides to stop killing or trying to kill. However touching such an agreement might be, it would also be somewhat disturbing, for one must always beware of an enemy who resorts so freely to tricks and traps of every kind. It was as well not to celebrate Christmas too obtrusively. Besides, I did not think we were the only ones keeping vigil at that hour.

From time to time we passed small groups of infantry, haggard, dusty, and heavily laden, marching in ranks with their arms slung, by threes or fours, without speaking, striding slowly, as though they were trying to measure the length of the road. Some of them were carrying curious objects fastened to sticks: pots or big cans, perhaps baskets. Where they were going or what they were doing we did not ask. Every man has his own job; if those fellows were going that way they had their orders, and nobody troubled himself about their object. All was well. The clattering of the Chasseurs on the uneven road lent a little life to the picture. Perhaps they were talking together; but, if so, it was in an undertone, a whisper almost.

And suddenly the enemy let us know that he was also

keeping watch. Far ahead of us, near C., a rocket went up into the clear sky and then fell slowly, very slowly, in the form of an intensely brilliant ball, lighting up all the surrounding country wonderfully. We knew them well, those formidable German rockets, which seemed as though they would never go out and shed a pallid and yet blinding light. We knew that as soon as they were lighted everybody who happened to be within range of the enemy's rifle fire had at once to lie flat on the ground, and not move or raise his head so long as the light was burning. Otherwise shots would be fired from all directions, mowing down the vegetation and cutting up the earth all around him. This time we were well outside the range, and we watched the dazzling star in front of us without halting.

"The shepherds' star," said G. solemnly.

Strange shepherds indeed must they have been who carried carbines as their crooks, and were provided with cartridges enough to send a hundred and twenty of their fellow-creatures into the next world. The star seemed to hang for a moment some yards from the ground; then slowly, slowly, as though exhausted by its effort, it fell to the ground and went out. The night seemed less clear and less diaphanous.

We had now reached the glass-works and it was there that we were to leave our cooks. No one would have supposed that this large factory lay idle, and that the hundreds of workmen employed there were dispersed. On the contrary, it seemed to have retained all the animation of the prosperous enterprise it had been before the war.

It was a large square of massive buildings, almost a miniature town, planted on the side of the canal, like an outlying bastion of the suburbs of R. The low white walls, crowned with tiles, had the stunted appearance of military works. But a nearer view gave rather the illusion of the life in a busy factory at night-time. The gateway opened on a courtyard, with furnace fires shining here and there. Shadowy forms passed backwards and forwards, enlivening the dim scene with the bustle of a hive. Men came out by fives or sixes, laden with different kinds of burdens, and disappeared into the darkness, making for mysterious goals. In front of the open gate other figures were unloading heavy cases from vans. These quondam glass-works were now a depôt for the Army Supply service, and a huge kitchen, which administered and fed the whole sector of trenches, of which ours formed a part.

The Germans knew this. So every day and many times a day their guns fired a few salvoes of shells on the huge quadrilateral. But our good troopers were none the worse. Instead of working in the large buildings, part of which had already been destroyed by shells, they utilised the vast basements of the factory. There were the stores, and there they had their kitchens, where they worked day and night to supply their comrades in the trenches with the hot abundant food which twice a day made them forget for a few minutes the hardships of the cold, the rain, and the mud.

Our column halted under the bleak wall. At the wide gateway a sentinel was on duty, standing motionless, muffled in a heavy grey cloak; and through it our cooks passed, disappearing into the darkness, under the guidance of the liaison orderly of the preceding detachment. Whilst waiting for his return from the journey through the labyrinth our Chasseurs had a short rest before beginning the most difficult part of their journey—the last stage on the way to the trenches we were to occupy.

I took the opportunity of talking with an infantry captain who was there, walking up and down with his face buried in a thick muffler and his hands in the pockets of his heavy overcoat, on the sleeves of which three small pieces of gold lace were just discernible.

"Eh bien, mon Capitaine! Anything new?"

"Oh! nothing, except my opinion that you will not be disturbed either to-day or to-morrow. Since yesterday evening they have not fired one shot, and they were singing hymns till midnight. You may be pretty sure they'll redouble their Oremus this Christmas night, so you may sleep soundly."

"Unless all this is merely a feint, and to-night ..."

"Yes, you're right, unless to-night ..."

The column started, and, guided by the liaison orderly, we followed the high-road for some hundred yards. The shells had transformed it into a series of gorges, peaks, ravines, and hills. We had to jump over big branches cut from the trees by the projectiles. It was a road that would not be a cheerful one on moonless nights. Fortunately for us, that particular night was extremely bright. Everything around us could be distinguished; we could even divine about fifteen hundred yards to our right the "solitary tree," the famous tree, standing alone in the middle of the vast bare plain, which marked the centre of our sector of trenches, and where I knew I should find the "dug-out" belonging to the officers of our regiment. I was very much tempted to jump the ditch at the side of the road and cut across the fields to the final point of our march. It would have taken about twenty minutes, and have saved us the long difficult journey through the communication trench. But our orders were very precise: we were not to take short cuts even on dark nights, much less on starlit nights. Our chiefs do well to be cautious on our behalf, for it is certain that, though fully alive to the danger of such a route, there was not one of my hundred fellows who would have hesitated to dash across country just to save himself a few hundred yards.

We came to the mouth of the approach trench, four or five huge steps cut in the chalky clay. The frost had made them slippery, and we had to keep close to the edge of the bank to avoid stumbling. Behind me I heard some of the men sliding down heavily, and a din of mess-tins rolling away amidst laughter and jokes. "A merry heart goes all the way," and I knew my Chasseurs would soon pick themselves up and make up for lost time. This was essential, for the approach trench had ramifications and unexpected cross-passages which might have led a laggard astray.

We went forward slowly. The communication trench was at right angles to the enemy's trenches. To prevent him from enfilading it with his shells, it had been cut in zigzags. And I hardly know of a more laborious method of progression than that of taking ten paces to the right, making a sharp turn, and then again taking ten paces to the left, and so on, in order to cover a distance which, as the crow flies, would not be more than fifteen hundred yards. The passage was so narrow that we touched the walls on either side. The moonlight could not reach the ground we trod on, and we stumbled incessantly over the holes and inequalities caused by the late rains and hardened by the frost. Now and again we slid over ice that had formed on the little pools through which our comrades had been paddling two days before. And this was some consolation for the severity of the frost, preferable a hundred times to the horrors of the rain.

At last we debouched into our trenches, where our predecessors were impatiently waiting for us. Two days and two nights is a long time to go without sleeping, without washing, without having any other view than the walls of earth that shut you in. They were all eager to go back over the same road they had come by two days before, to get to their horses again, their quarters, their friends—in short, their home. So we found them quite ready to go, blankets rolled up and slung over their shoulders, and knapsacks in their places under their cloaks.

Whilst the non-commissioned officers of each squadron went to relieve the men at the listening posts, I brushed past the men lined up against the wall, and went towards the "solitary tree," which seemed to be stretching out its gaunt arms to protect our retreat. I had to turn to the right in a narrow passage which went round the tree, and ended in three steep steps cut in the earth, down which I had to go to reach the dug-out.

My old friend La G. was waiting for me at the bottom of this den, stretched on two chairs, warming his feet at a tiny iron stove perched upon a heap of bricks. By the light of the one candle he looked imposing and serious. His tawny beard, which he had allowed to grow since the war, spread like a fan over his chest, and gave him a look of Henri IV. I knew that this formidable exterior concealed the merriest companion and the most delightful sly joker that ever lived. So I was not much impressed by his thoughtful brow and his dreamy eye.

"Well, what's the news?" I asked.

"We are all freezing," he replied.

I rather suspected it. Besides this fact, which we had discovered before him, La G. could only confirm what the infantry captain had told me shortly before:

"You are going to have a most restful night, my dear fellow; and I advise you to have a Christmas manger arranged at the foot of the 'solitary tree,' and at midnight to sing 'Christians, awake,' in chorus.... We know some hymns as well as the Germans."

I had no lack of desire to put this proposal into action, but such pious customs as these would not perhaps have been quite in harmony with the tactical ideas of our commanding officer. Still I promised La G. I would do my best for the realisation of his dream.

"Good-bye and good luck!" he said.

"Good-bye," I replied.

And he went away into the darkness. At the end of the little passage that led to the trench I could see the men who had just been relieved passing in single file going towards the communication trench by which we had come. Their dark forms defiled in closely and rapidly. Having completed their task, they were happy to be free to get back to their squadrons, and as they passed they cracked their jokes at the others who had to stay. These answered back, but not in the most amiable manner. Then, little by little, silence settled down upon the scene. Every man was at his post: some kept watch, others walked about at the bottom of the trench or busied themselves with repairing or improving the indifferent shelters their predecessors had left them.

G. had gone to take the watch on which the junior officers of the units defending the sector relieved each other every three hours. So there I was alone, alone in the midst of my brave Chasseurs, with the duty of guarding those five hundred yards of trenches—a very small piece at that time of the immense French line. Behind us thousands of our fellows were sleeping in perfect confidence, relying upon the thin rampart we formed in front of them; and farther away still there were millions of Frenchmen and Frenchwomen, who, under their family roof or under that of their hosts, were resting in peace because of our sleepless nights, our limbs stiffened by the cold, our carbines pointed through the loopholes of the trenches.

Thus were we to celebrate the merry festival of Christmas. There was no doubt that far away among those who were keeping the sacred vigil more than one would think of us and sympathise with us.... No doubt many a one among us would feel a touch of sadness that evening, thinking of his home. But none, not one, I felt sure, would wish to quit his post to get away from the Front. Military honour!

glorious legacy of our ancestors! Who could have foreseen that it would be implanted so naturally and so easily in the young souls of our soldiers? Within their youthful bodies the same hearts were already beating as those of the immortal veterans of the epic days of France. Men are fashioned by war.

Ten o'clock came on Christmas Eve to find that our day had passed in almost absolute calm. It had been a glorious winter day, a day of bright sunshine and pure clear air. The Germans had hardly fired at all. A few cannon-shots only had replied to our artillery, which let off its heavy guns every now and then upon their positions from the heights behind us.

And then night came. B. and I had just finished our frugal meal. We had promised to pay a visit to the Territorials who occupied the trenches right and left of ours. Our Chasseurs had been posted in that particular section so that in case of attack they might form a solid base for the Territorials to rely upon. They did not conceal their confidence in our men or their admiration for them; and their officers had no scruples in asking for our advice when difficult cases arose. In fact, that very afternoon the captain commanding the company to our right had come to my dug-out to arrange with me about the patrols that had to be sent that night in advance of the line.

Wrapped in our cloaks, we came out of our warm retreat. The night was just like the previous one, starlit, bright, and frosty, a true Christmas night for times of peace. In our trenches one half of the men were awake, in obedience to orders. Carbines were loaded and placed in the loopholes, and the guns were trained upon the enemy. In front of us, at the end of the narrow passages which led out to the listening posts, I knew that our sentries were alert with eye and ear, crouching in their holes in pairs. No one could approach the broad network of wire which protected us without being immediately perceived and shot. At the bottom of the trenches the men on watch were talking softly together and stamping on the ground to combat the intense cold.

Those who were at rest, lying close together at the bottom of the little dug-outs they had made for themselves in the bank, were sleeping or trying to sleep. More than one of them had succeeded, for resounding snores could be heard behind the blankets, pieces of tent canvas and sacking, and all the various rags with which they had ingeniously stuffed up the entrances to their rustic alcoves. One wondered how they could have overcome the sufferings the cold must have caused them so far as to be able to sleep calmly. The five months of war had hardened their bodies and accustomed them to face cold, heat, rain, dust, or mud, with impunity. In this hard school, better than in any other, men of iron are fashioned, who last out a whole campaign and are capable of the supreme effort when the hour comes.

We arrived at the Territorials' trench.

"Bon-soir, mon cher camarade."

It was the Second-Lieutenant whom I met at the entrance. He was a man of forty-two, thin, pale, and bearded. In the shadow his eyes shone strangely. Under the skirts of his great-coat he had his hands buried in his trouser pockets. His elbows stuck out from his body, his knees were bent, his teeth chattered, and he was gently knocking his heels together.

"It isn't warm, eh?" I asked.

"Oh, no; and then, you see, this sort of work is hardly the thing for fellows of our age. Our blood isn't warm enough, and, however you cover yourself up, there's always a chink by which the cold gets in. The worst of all is one's hands and feet; and there's nothing to be done for it. Wouldn't it be much better to trust to us, give us the order to fix bayonets and drive those Boches out of their trenches over there? You'd see if the Territorials couldn't do it as well as the Regulars.... And then one would have a chance of getting warm."

I felt sure that he spoke the truth, and that his opinion was shared by the majority of his companions. But our good comrades of the Territorial Force have no conception of the vigour, the suppleness, and of the fulness of youth required to charge up to the enemy's line under concentrated fire and to cut the complex network of barbed wire that bars the road. Our chiefs were well advised in placing these troops where they were, in those lines of trenches scientifically constructed and protected, where their courage and tenacity would be invaluable in case of attack, and where they would know better than any others how to carry out the orders given to us: "Hold on till death." Leave to the young soldiers the sublime and perilous task of rushing upon the enemy when he is hidden behind the shelter of his fougades, his parapets, and his artificial brambles; and entrust to the brave Territorials the more obscure but not less glorious work of mounting guard along our front.

I could make them out in the moonlight, standing silent and alert, in groups of two or three. Perched on the ledge of earth which raised them to the height of the parapet, they had their eyes wide open in the darkness, looking towards the enemy. Their loaded rifles were placed in front of them, between two clods of hardened earth. They neither complained nor uttered a word, but suffered nobly. They understand that they must. Ah! where now were the fine tirades of pothouse orators and public meetings? Where now were the oaths to revolt, the solemn denials and the blasphemies pronounced against the Fatherland? All was forgotten, wiped out from the records. If we could have questioned those men who stood there shivering, chilled to the bone, watching over the safety of the country, not one of them, certainly, would have confessed that he was ever one of the renegades of yore. And yet if one were to search among the bravest, among the most resigned, among the best, thousands of them would be discovered. Heaven grant that this miracle, wrought by the war, may be prolonged far beyond the days of the struggle, and then we shall not think that our brothers' blood has been spilt in vain.

We brushed past them, but they did not even turn round. Eyes, mind, and will were absorbed in the dark mystery of the silent landscape stretching out before them. But the night, though it was so bright, gave everything a strange appearance; transformed all living things and increased their size; made the stones, the stacks, and the trees move, as it seemed to our weary eyes; cast fitful shadows where there were none; and made us hear murmurs which sounded like the muffled tramp of troops marching cautiously. Those men watched because they felt that there was always the danger of a surprise attack, of a sudden rush of Teutons who had crawled up through the grass of the fields. They had piled on their backs empty sacks, blankets, and old rags, for warmth, and wound their mufflers two or three times round their necks; they had taken all possible precautions for carrying out their duty to the very last. And although our hearts had been hardened by the unprecedented miseries of this war, we were seized with pity and admiration. Presently one of them turned round and said to us:

"Hallo! They are lighting up over there now."

I jumped up on to the ledge and saw, in fact, lights shining in three different places some way off. After looking attentively I guessed the meaning of this quite unusual illumination in the rear of the trenches. The lights came from some large fir-trees, placed there under cover of night, and beautifully lighted up. With my glasses I could make them out distinctly, and even the figures dancing round them; and we could hear their voices and shouts of merriment. How well they had arranged the whole thing! They had even gone as far as to light up their Christmas trees with electricity, so as to prevent our gunners from using them as an easy target. In fact, every few minutes all the lights on a tree were suddenly put out, and only appeared some minutes afterwards.

We had thrilled instinctively. Suddenly there arose, all over the wide plain, solemn and melodious singing. We still remembered singing of a similar kind we had recently heard at Bixschoote on a tragic occasion; and here were the same tuneful voices again, singing a hymn of the same kind as those they sang further to the north before shouting their hurrahs for the attack. But we did not fear anything of that kind now. We had the impression that this singing was not a special prayer in front of our little sector of trenches, but that it was general, and extended without limits over the whole of our provinces violated by the enemy: over Champagne, Lorraine, and Picardy, resounding from the North Sea to the Rhine.

The Territorial trench was full of noiseless animation. The men came up out of their little dug-outs without a word, and the whole company was soon perched upon the ledge. There was a silence among our men, as if each man felt uneasy or perhaps jealous of what was going on over there. Then, as if to order, along the line of the German trenches other hymns rang out, and one choir seemed to answer the other. The singing became general. Quite close to us, in the trenches themselves, in the distance, round their brightly lighted trees, to the right, to the left, it resounded, softened by the distance. What a stirring, nay, grandiose, impression those hymns made, floating over the vast field of death! I felt intuitively that all this had been arranged long before, that they might celebrate their Christmas with religious calm and peace.

At any other time, no doubt, many a clumsy joke would have been made, and no little abuse hurled at the singers. But all that has been changed. I divined some regret among our brave fellows that we were not taking part in a similar festival. Was it not Christmas Eve? Had we not been obliged by our duty to give up the delightful family gathering which reunites us yearly around the symbolic Yule-log? This year our mothers, our sisters, and our children were keeping up the time-honoured and pious custom alone. Why did not our larger family of to-day join in singing together around lighted fir-trees? Our Territorials did not speak; but their thoughts flew away from the trenches, and the regrets of all were fused in a common feeling of melancholy.

Little by little the singing died away, and absolute silence fell once more upon the country.

* * * * *

I went with G. as far as his watch-post. He had to resume his duty as officer of the watch from eleven o'clock in the evening to two o'clock in the morning. The post consisted of a kind of small blockhouse, strongly built and protected by two casemates with machine-guns placed so as to command the enemy's trenches. A machine-gunner was always on guard, and could call the others, at the slightest alarm, to work the gun. These men were quartered in a kind of tunnel hollowed out close by, and at the first signal would have been ready to open fire with their terrible engines of destruction. In the centre of the block-house a padded sentry-box was arranged made of a number of sand-bags, in which, by means of a loophole, the officer of the watch could observe the whole sector entrusted to us; and by means of a telephone station, close at hand, he could communicate at any moment with the commander of the sector at the glass-works.

G. had put on the goatskin coat handed to him by the officer he relieved. This officer was a Second-Lieutenant of Territorials, and looked completely frozen.

"Here, my dear fellow," he said, "I leave you the goatskin provided for the use of the officer on duty. I should have liked to give it you well warmed, but I feel like an icicle myself."

G. was nevertheless glad to have it. After wishing him good luck, I left him to get back to my hut, for, in spite of my cloak, the frost was taking hold of me too. The faithful Wattrelot had done his best to keep our little stove going. Profiting by La G.'s example, I stretched myself on two chairs, with my feet towards the fire. I gradually got warmer, and at the same time somewhat melancholy. What a curious Christmas Eve! Certainly I had never passed one in such a place. The walls were made of a greyish, friable earth, which still showed the marks of the pick that had been used for the excavation. The furniture was simple and not very comfortable. At the back was the bed, made out of a little straw already well tossed over by a number of sleepers. This straw was kept in by a plank fixed to the ground and forming the side of the modest couch. Against the wall, opposite the stove, was the table. This table, which had to serve for writing and feeding, and perhaps for a game of cards, this table, which was required to fill the part of all the tables of all the rooms of any house, was, strange to say, a night-table. I wondered who had brought it there, and who had chosen it. But, such as it was, it served its purpose pretty well. We used it for dinner, and found it almost comfortable, and upon it I signed a number of reports and orders.

Together with the two chairs, the stove, the bed, and some nails to hang my clothes on, that table completed the furniture of the "home" where I meditated on that December night. The candle, stuck in a bottle, flickered at the slightest breath, and threw strange shadows on the walls.

It was the hour of solitude and silence, the hour of meditation and of sadness too now and then. That evening dark thoughts were flying about in that smoky den, assailing me in crowds, and taking possession of my mind; I could not drive them away. It was one of those moments—those very fleeting moments!—when courage seems to fail, and one gives way with a kind of bitter satisfaction. I remembered that months and months had passed since I had seen any of those belonging to me, and I conjured up in my mind the picture of the Christmas Eve they were keeping, too, at that same hour, at the other end of France. And the dear, good friends I had left in Paris and in Rouen—where were they at that moment? What were they doing? Were they thinking of me? How I should have liked to enjoy the wonderful power possessed by certain heroes in the Arabian Nights, which would have allowed me to see at that moment a vision of the loved ones far away. Were they talking about me, sitting together round the fire? I thought that this war had been a splendid thing to us Chasseurs as long as we were fighting as cavalry, scouring the plains, searching the woods, galloping in advance of our infantry, and bringing them information which enabled them to deal their blows or parry those of the enemy, trying to come up with the Prussian cavalry which fled before us. But this trench warfare, this warfare in which one stays for days and days in the same position, in which ground is gained yard by yard, in which artifice tries to outdo artifice, in which each side clings to the ground it has won, digs into it, buries itself in it, and dies in it sooner than give it up! What warfare for cavalry!

We have devoted ourselves to it with all our hearts, and the chiefs who have had us under their orders have never failed to commend us; but at times we feel very weary, and during inaction and solitude our imaginations begin to work. Then we recall our regiment in full gallop over field and plain; we hear the clank of swords and bits; we see once more the flash of the blades, the motley line of the horses; we evoke the well-known figures of our chiefs on their chargers. That night my mind became more restless than ever before; it broke loose, it leapt away, and lived again the unforgettable stages of this war: Charleroi, Guise, the Marne, the defence of the Jaulgonne bridge, Montmirail, Reims, ... Belgium, Bixschoote; and then it fell back into the gloomy dug-out where the flame of the single candle traced disquieting shadows on the wall.

Suddenly a cold breath of air blew into my retreat. The door opened abruptly, and at the top of the steps a man, stooping over the floor of the passage, called me in an undertone:

"Mon Lieutenant, come and see.... Something is happening...."

With a bound, I sprang from my shelter and climbed up the ledge.

"Listen, mon Lieutenant ."

That night in the trenches was destined to overwhelm me with astonishment, and this one surpassed all that I could imagine. I should like to be able to impart the extraordinary impression I felt; but one would have to have been there that night to be capable of realising it. Over that vast and silent plain, in which everything seemed to sleep and where no other sound was heard, there resounded from afar a voice whose notes, in spite of the distance, reached our ears. What an extraordinary thing it was! That song, vibrating through the boundless night, made our hearts beat and stirred us more than the most perfectly ordered concert given by the most famous singers.

And it was another hymn, unknown to us, coming from the German trenches far away on our left. The singer must have been standing out in the fields on the edge of their line; he must have been moving, coming towards us, and passing slowly along all the enemy's positions, for his voice came gradually nearer, and became louder and clearer. Every now and then it ceased, and then hundreds of other voices responded in chorus with some phrases which formed the refrain of the hymn. Then the soloist began again and came still nearer to us. He must have come from a considerable distance, for our Chasseurs had already heard him some time before they decided to call me. Who could this man have been, who must have been sent along the front of the troops to pray, whilst each German company waited for him, so as to join with him in prayer? Some minister, no doubt, who had come to remind the soldiers of the sanctity of that night and the solemnity of the hour.

Soon we heard the voice coming from the trenches straight in front of us. In spite of the brightness of the night, we could not distinguish the singer, for the two lines at that point were four hundred yards apart. But he was certainly not hiding himself, for his deep voice would never have sounded so rich and clear to us had he been singing at the bottom of their trenches. Again it ceased. And then the Germans directly in front of us, the soldiers occupying the works opposite ours, those men whom we were bound to kill so soon as they appeared, and whose duty it was to shoot us so soon as we showed ourselves—those men calmly took up the refrain of the hymn, with its sweet and mysterious words. They too must have come to the edge of their trench and struck up their hymn with their faces towards us, for their notes came to us clearly and distinctly.

I looked along the line of our trench. All our men too were awake and looking on. They had all got on to the ledge, and several had left the trench and were in the field, listening to the unexpected concert. No one was offended by it; no one laughed at it. Rather was there a trace of regret in the attitudes and the faces of those who were nearest to me. And yet it would have been such a simple matter to put an end to that scene; a volley fired by the troop there, and it would all stop, and drop back into the quiet of other nights. But nobody thought of such a thing. There was not one of our Chasseurs who would not have considered it a sacrilege to fire upon those praying soldiers. We felt indeed that there are hours when one can forget that one is there to kill. This would not prevent us from doing our duty immediately afterwards.

The voice drew farther away, and retreated slowly and majestically towards the trenches situated at the place known as the "Troopers of C.'s" ground, where our two lines approached each other within a distance of fifty yards. How much more touching the sight must have been from there! I wished my post had been in that direction, so that I might have been present at the scene, might have heard the words and distinguished the figure of the pastor walking along the parapets made for hurling out death, and blessing those who the next day might be no more.

Ping! A shot was heard....

The stupid bullet which had perhaps found its mark? At once there was dead silence, not a cry, not an oath, not a groan. Some one had thought he was doing well by firing on that man. A pity! We should gain nothing by preventing them from keeping Christmas in their own way, and it would have been a nobler thing to reserve our blows for other hecatombs. I know that the barbarians would not have hesitated had they been in our place, and that so many of our priests had fallen under their strokes that they could not reasonably have reproached us. There are people who will say that our hatred should embrace everything German; that we should be implacable towards everything bearing that name, and spare none of the execrated race which has been the cause of so many tears, so much blood, so much mourning. Never mind!... I think in this case it would have been better not to have shot....

A shot fired, not far from us, on our left brought me up from my shelter. It seemed strange after the complete calm of that night. It was seven o'clock. The sun was magnificent, and had already bathed the deserted plain, the fields, the heights of S., and the ruined village. In the distance, towards the east, the towers of the cathedral of R. stood out proudly against the golden sky. I looked and saw all my Chasseurs standing on the ledges watching with interest a scene which seemed to be going on in front of the trenches occupied on our left by the Territorials.

I got up by the side of one of them, and he explained to me what was happening.

"Mon Lieutenant, it's the infantry fellows who have just killed a hare that ran between the two lines, and they're going to fetch it...."

And in fact I saw this strange sight: two men had gone out in full daylight from their trenches and were advancing with hesitating steps towards the enemy's. Behind them were a hundred inquisitive heads, looking out above the embrasures arranged between the sacks of earth. A few soldiers, who had come out of the trench, were even sitting on the bank of chalky earth. It was certainly such a scene as I had hardly expected to witness. What was the captain of the company occupying the trench doing?

But my astonishment became stupefaction when I saw the hundreds of heads that fringed the enemy's trenches. I at once sent G. and a non-commissioned officer with the following order to all our men:

"No one is to show himself.... Every man to his fighting post!... Carbines loaded and ready to fire!"

The Germans opposite became suspicious on seeing our line so silent, and no man showing himself; they, too, waited on the alert behind their loopholes. But along the rest of their front their men kept on coming out from their trenches unarmed, and making merry and friendly gestures. I became uneasy, and wondered how this unexpected comedy might end. Ought I to have those men fired upon who were not quite opposite to us, and whose opponents seemed rather inclined to make a Christmas truce?

Our two infantrymen had come to the spot where the hare had fallen, very nearly half-way between the French and the German lines. One of them stooped down and got up again proudly brandishing his victim in the enemy's faces. At once there was a burst of applause from the German lines. They called out: "Kameraden! Kameraden!"

This was going too far. I saw two unarmed Prussians leave their trench and come forward, with their hands raised towards the two Frenchmen, so I consulted G.: "Ought we to fire? I confess it would be rather unpleasant for me to order our fellows to fire upon these unarmed men. On the other hand, can we allow the least intercourse between the barbarous nation that is still treading our soil and our good brothers-in-arms who are pouring out their blood every day to reconquer it?"

Fortunately, the officer who commanded the Saint Thierry artillery, and who had observed this scene with his glasses, spared me a decision which would have been painful to me.

Pong! Pong! Pong! Pong!

Four shells passed, hissing, over our heads, and burst with

admirable precision two hundred yards above the German trenches. The artillery officer seemed to have placed with a delicate hand the four little white puffs of smoke which, equidistant from each other, appeared to mark out the bounds in the heavens of the frontier line he wished to forbid the enemy to pass on the earth. The Germans did not fail to understand this graceful warning. With cries of rage and protest, they ran back to their shelters, and our Frenchmen did the same.

And, as though to mark the intentional kindness of what he had just done, hardly had the last of the spiked helmets disappeared behind the parapets, when again the same hissing noise was heard, and, pong! pong! pong! pong! four shells dropped, this time full upon the whitish line formed along the green plain by the upturned earth of their trenches. In the midst of the smoke, earth and rubbish of all kinds were seen flying. Our Chasseurs cried "Bravo!" Everyone felt that the best solution had been found, and rejoiced at this termination of the brief Christmas truce.

And now our minds were free to rejoice in the great day itself in company with our good troopers. In the night there had arrived, well packed in smart hampers, the bottles of champagne which Major B. had presented to his men, and we were looking forward to the time, only a few hours hence, when the soup would be upon the table, and we should keep our Christmas by letting off the corks in the direction of the German trenches.

Our young fellow-officers were already anticipating this peaceful salvo—which would certainly be heard by the enemy.

ALSO FROM LEONAUR

AVAILABLE IN SOFTCOVER OR HARDCOVER WITH DUST JACKET

EW2 EYEWITNESS TO WAR SERIES

CAPTAIN OF THE 95th (Rifles) *by Jonathan Leach*

An officer of Wellington's Sharpshooters during the Peninsular, South of France and Waterloo Campaigns of the Napoleonic Wars.

SOFTCOVER : **ISBN 1-84677-001-7**
HARDCOVER : **ISBN 1-84677-016-5**

WF1 THE WARFARE FICTION SERIES

NAPOLEONIC WAR STORIES

by Sir Arthur Quiller-Couch

Tales of soldiers, spies, battles & Sieges from the Peninsular & Waterloo campaigns

SOFTCOVER : **ISBN 1-84677-003-3**
HARDCOVER : **ISBN 1-84677-014-9**

EW1 EYEWITNESS TO WAR SERIES

RIFLEMAN COSTELLO *by Edward Costello*

The adventures of a soldier of the 95th (Rifles) in the Peninsular & Waterloo Campaigns of the Napoleonic wars.

SOFTCOVER : **ISBN 1-84677-000-9**
HARDCOVER : **ISBN 1-84677-018-1**

MC1 THE MILITARY COMMANDERS SERIES

JOURNALS OF ROBERT ROGERS OF THE RANGERS *by Robert Rogers*

The exploits of Rogers & the Rangers in his own words during 1755-1761 in the French & Indian War.

SOFTCOVER : **ISBN 1-84677-002-5**
HARDCOVER : **ISBN 1-84677-010-6**

AVAILABLE ONLINE AT
www.leonaur.com
AND OTHER GOOD BOOK STORES

Printed in the United Kingdom
by Lightning Source UK Ltd.
116206UKS00001B/333

9 781846 771118